Peter G. Stromberg
received his Ph.D. in anthropology
from Stanford University and was a
postdoctoral fellow at the University
of California at San Diego and the
University of California at Berkeley.
He now teaches at the University of
Arizona.

Symbols of Community

THE ANTHROPOLOGY OF FORM AND MEANING

SYMBOLS OF COMMUNITY

The Cultural System of a Swedish Church

Peter G. Stromberg

The University of Arizona Press
Tucson

About the Author

PETER STROMBERG is a cultural anthropologist who received his
Ph.D. from Stanford University. He has taught in the anthropology
department at Stanford, the sociology department at the University
of California at Berkeley, and the anthropology department at the
University of Arizona in Tucson. As a Fulbright scholar in Stockholm in the 1970s, he had the opportunity to become acquainted with
his Swedish heritage and to conduct the research on which this book
is based.

THE UNIVERSITY OF ARIZONA PRESS

Copyright © 1986
The Arizona Board of Regents
All Rights Reserved

This book was set in 10/12 Linotron 202 Bembo.
Manufactured in the U.S.A.

Library of Congress Cataloging in Publication Data

Stromberg, Peter G.
Symbols of community.

Bibliography: p.
Includes index.
1. Culture—Case studies. 2. Commitment (Psychology)
—Case studies. 3. Community—Case studies.
4. Social groups—Case studies. 5. Immanuelskyrkan
(Stockholm, Sweden)—Case studies. I. Title.
HM101.S84   1986   306′.6   85-30229

ISBN 0-8165-0967-0 (alk. paper)

For my mother,
Beatrice Stromberg

Contents

The next task would be rather to show the significance of ascetic rationalism, which has only been touched in the foregoing sketch, for the content of practical social ethics, thus for the types of organization and the functions of social groups from the conventicle to the State.

MAX WEBER
The Protestant Ethic
and the Spirit of Capitalism

Preface

This book is an argument about how culture works in a modern, complex society. The argument is based on an extended example, a study of a Swedish church called Immanuel Church or, in Swedish, *Immanuelskyrkan*. I learned about this church in sixteen months of research in Sweden, talking to the men and women of Immanuel Church, attending their meetings, and studying the history of the group.

In writing a work of this scope, an author receives so much help from so many people that an adequate job of acknowledgment is impossible. Therefore, I will mention specifically only the most obvious of my debts here; I trust that the many people who have contributed in some way to this project will accept my general thanks as graciously as they offered their assistance when I needed it.

I must first express my gratitude to the men and women of *Immanuelskyrkan* in Stockholm, who were without exception interested and encouraging, and usually delighted that I had come from America to study their church. Their simple friendliness and unquestioning acceptance was a primary factor in making my stay in Sweden such a pleasant one. Above all, I would like to thank my friend and research assistant Roland Strand; our many long discussions were perhaps the most vital part of the process whereby I gained an intellectual and emotional perspective on the members of Immanuel Church.

[xi]

Second, certain of my friends and teachers have contributed tirelessly to this project, and I would like to acknowledge their help. These are Christopher Crocker, Roy D'Andrade, Renato Rosaldo, the late Michelle Rosaldo, David Sapir, and Ann Swidler.

In addition, my thanks go to the Social Science Research Council, the Fulbright Program, the American-Scandinavian Foundation, and the National Institute of Mental Health for providing the financial assistance that made this study possible.

Finally, my thanks to Ingmar Bergman and *The New Yorker* magazine for their permission to quote several passages from Mr. Bergman's short story, "Cries and Whispers," which originally appeared in that publication.

Parts of the second chapter of this book first appeared in the journal *Ethnos* (volume 48, pp. 69 – 84). Parts of the fourth and fifth chapters originally appeared as a paper in the *American Ethnologist* (volume 8, number 3, 1981). These sections appear by permission.

PETER G. STROMBERG

Symbols of Community

1

Consensus and Commitment

Members of Immanuel Church in Stockholm took their seats on a Sunday morning in the late spring of 1975 to hear what they knew would be the final sermon preached by their well-loved pastor, Nils Mjönes. Mjönes had been absent from the church for many weeks previous to that morning, for he was dying of cancer. He returned at the end of the long Swedish winter, however, to say his final good-by to the congregation.

His sermon was short and very simple that morning. He began:

> As you know, the theme for today is "Walking with the Risen Lord." I am reminded of an old Chinese tale—which you might know—about an artist who painted a landscape, one of those typical Chinese scenes with mountains, streams, and trees. He painted a wonderful piece of art, full of life and beauty. When he had finished his work—so the story goes—he rose and walked straight into that living landscape. I wish I could, to use Paul's words, portray Christ so vividly before your eyes that my description would be like this piece of Chinese art. I wish I could portray the living Christ, and then disappear into his fellowship.

The paradox in this Chinese tale is the "perfect picture," so perfect one can walk into it. If perfect, it is no picture. But the tale causes the listener to forget that principle for a moment and thus to bring the concepts of image and reality closer to one another than they normally stand. In the unstable compound formed by their merger, that which exists is not distinguished from that which is conceived. Faith is reality.

Although it is said that the Chinese artist walked into his picture, Nils Mjönes expressed the wish that he could *disappear* into his portrayal of Christ. The slight variation is of course not accidental; all those present knew the pastor was soon to disappear. These words, then, can be taken as Nils Mjönes's reflections on his own death. By referring to his death in the terms of the story of the Chinese artist, he offers a new conception of mortality.

Think of my death, he says, as occurring at the miraculous juncture between image and reality. Usually Christians think of that point in terms of an *appearance,* for it is central to their faith that God once became a tangible part of this world. It is that which is important, says Nils Mjönes; if we believe that God does become reality, we can conceive our inevitable disappearance as merely crossing the boundary God has already opened.

Nils Mjönes's parable is a variation on the theme of this study, the idea of grace at Immanuel Church. He, like most believers at Immanuel Church, found in this complex, even paradoxical, idea a means to conceive of his existence in a meaningful way. His story is testimony to the continuing attempt among believers at this church to retain their conviction that it is not only in the distant past that image and reality merged into one another; rather, such processes occur here and now in their own lives. In the moments when the tenets of their faith become real, in the moments when the words of the Bible seem to merge with their experience and take on a new meaning, church members believe they have seen image become reality; they have experienced grace.

In the most spare formulation, one could say that "grace" is the word believers at Immanuel Church use to refer to the process whereby the tenets of their faith become meaningful for the faithful. As such, grace is a compelling object of study for any cultural scientist, a person whose job, after all, is to study how culture is implicated in social life. Note, however, that in adopting such a focus I am taking a perspective on life at Immanuel Church that believers there might regard as peculiar; it is grace as a cultural phenomenon, not as a religious one, that interests me in this book.[1]

In other words, this is a book of social science—and in an important sense a book *about* social science—and not a book about God. I have chosen to write a book about the idea of grace at Immanuel Church because I think that such a case study will have wider implications for the way social scientists think about a cultural system such as a religion in a modern society. Concisely expressed, my point is this: anthropologists and some sociologists have a loosely organized, although deeply entrenched, set of ideas about how the symbols, conceptions, and ideas used by a group of people influence the lives of those people. This set of ideas comprises an important part of what is generally termed the "culture concept." I want to argue that certain elements of this culture concept are incoherent and that the process of grace—which is, again, a clear example of how cultural symbols enter into the lives of the men and women who use them—is a good place to begin to think about how to clarify certain of these incoherencies.

Undertaking any discussion on the theory of culture is a somewhat daunting task, in the first place because the term is used in any number of ways in social science. This situation renders it immensely difficult to engage the anthropological profession in a discussion about just what culture is and what it does; as in guerrilla warfare, one cannot locate the enemy, much less fight him or her. The one thing that seems to be a point of agreement is that culture is an enormously significant phenomenon, an idea that has dominated the "intellectual landscape" of the twentieth century (see Geertz 1973: 3).

Unfortunately, this conviction of significance has evidently led to a certain complacency about the continued need to refine the concept. The tendency—which has now spread from anthropology throughout the social sciences, history, and the humanities—is to write as if "culture" had a widely accepted and unproblematic meaning. For example, authors often argue as if elements of the culture of some society can be safely assumed to be evenly distributed and similarly interpreted across the entire social group. In the currently canonical formulation: "Culture is a system of shared symbols and meanings." This phrase is intoned with sincerity in almost every corner of academic life, in spite of the fact that, when pressed, no anthropologist or sociologist will actually maintain that culture is completely and evenly shared in a society (see Swartz 1982: 315). As will be noted below, it *is* in fact commonly held that culture is widely (although not completely) shared in social groups, but this is a very different sort of claim—with very different implications—than that culture is completely shared.[2]

Another problem in undertaking a general discussion of culture is vocabulary. A vocabulary that makes discriminations among different kinds of culture is utterly nonexistent. The hoary convention, propped up by a century of anthropological tradition, is to assume that culture is the sum of the ideational, symbolic, or customary (or whatever) resources available to a social group. There is therefore an almost complete lack of acknowledgment in the literature that different systems that are undoubtedly cultural—say, myths, moral strictures, and the grammar of the language spoken in some society—may enter into social life in very different ways. (For example, a myth may be subject to reflection in a way a moral stricture is not, a moral stricture may be avoidable in a way a rule of grammar is not, and so on.) Instead, authors plunge bravely into a discussion of the social significance of "culture," ignoring the fact that different cultural systems may have different sorts of significance, both for the men and women who use them and for the maintenance of the social order.

The cultural system described in the following pages is a clear example of a particular sort of culture that is of tremendous significance in modern society, the cultural system whose adherents in some sense have *chosen* to accept that system.[3] Such systems, of which religions and political beliefs are the most often invoked examples, are sometimes called "ideologies," a term that entails a host of well-known problems. Therefore I will avoid that term and coin one of my own. For reasons that I will explain below, I call such a system a *commitment* system. Much of what follows can be seen as an attempt to work out the implications of this sort of cultural system for a general theory of culture.

Such an attempt would be much simpler were there an already existent general theory of culture to draw upon, criticize, and refine. However, there is no such theory. Perhaps as a result of the difficulties in discussing the term, cultural scientists have yet to produce an authoritative account of how "culture" fits into the broader framework of fundamental questions about society. Does the immense significance of culture follow from its role in sustaining social order? There is, in other words, an assumption underlying much of social thought that "during the time men live without a common power to keep them all in awe, they are in that condition which is called war, and such a war as is of every man against every man." (Hobbes 1958 [orig. 1651]: 106; cf. Parsons 1968 88ff.) Culture is often suggested as such a power. Or is the point rather that culture, like language, is a symbolic system so fundamental to human functioning that it virtually *constitutes* our mental faculties? Or is culture really not so significant after all—at least as an actual force in the social world—as Clifford Geertz (1973: 14) seems to assert when he writes: "culture is not a power, something to which social events, behaviors, institutions, or processes can be causally attributed; it is a context, something within which they can be intelligibly...described."

In the current work, I have tried to formulate a number of clear questions about how the cultural system at Immanuel Church, a system of commitment, actually works in ordering social life in that group. In what— if any—sense is culture *shared* throughout the group? Can culture be said to order or influence the behavior of individual actors? If so, how? Does culture contribute to the cohesion or solidarity of the social group in any discernible fashion?[4]

To repeat, my answers to these questions will be based on the observation of one type of cultural system, a system of commitment. I regard it as probable that other sorts of cultural systems work differently in social life from the one I will describe. Since I wish to call into question the conventional assumption that "culture" refers to a well-defined and coherent sociological category, I do not intend my description of "culture as commitment" as a new general model for the operation of culture. Rather, I intend such a description as a contribution to the larger task of building a more differentiated and precise approach to culture.

The conventional way of thinking about culture, which is based largely on anthropological studies of "primitive" societies, offers the following answers to the questions I have just posed: First, and most important, it is assumed that, yes, culture is a system of signs, or ideas, or objects that is widely if not completely shared in a social group. Second, and in a loose sense corollary to the first point, culture does influence culture-bearers, probably by constituting the limits of conception, by defining what is thinkable. More directly derived from the assumption of sharing is the answer to the third question: Culture constitutes solidarity in a group because it is the fact of a shared culture that defines a social group.

I will term this set of interlocking assumptions the "culture as consensus" perspective. This perspective takes as the model of culture the small-scale, presumably isolated societies which anthropologists have made it their special task to study. Although views of "primitive" society have changed radically in the past century, the essential mechanism of the place of culture in social life in such communities is today surprisingly little changed from the following (uncharacteristically nonsensical) description by Emile Durkheim (1915: 18):

> The group has an intellectual and moral conformity of which we find but rare examples in the more advanced societies. Everything is common to all. Movements are stereotyped; everybody performs the same ones in the same circumstances, and this conformity of conduct only translates the conformity of thought. Every mind being drawn into the same eddy, the individual type nearly confounds itself with that of the race.

Durkheim, of course, did not use the word "culture" in anything like its modern sense; what is quoted here merely reflects his incautious opinion about the nature of social life in conditions of what he at one point in his career called "mechanical solidarity." Although one would be hard pressed to find a contemporary scholar who would endorse Durkheim's conception of human action in "primitive" society, the underlying logic of his statement is in fact completely compatible with the modern conception of culture as it is commonly used, what I have called "culture as consensus." As in the set of assumptions described above, Durkheim attributes (1) a cognitive unity to the group which issues in (2) uniform action. Finally, (3) Durkheim conceives the society at this level as *constituted by* this shared consciousness. As

Anthony Giddens (1971: 76) has summarized this view: "The tribe as a whole forms a 'society' because it is a cultural unity: because the members of the various clan groups all adhere to the same set of common beliefs and sentiments."

Here Giddens introduces the word Durkheim did not use, but the anachronism is more insightful than distorting. The three interlocking components of determinism, consensus, and cohesion—so obvious in the passage from Durkheim—are, less obviously but just as certainly, the machinery that throbs at the center of the modern culture concept. It goes without saying that the modern version of culture as consensus lacks what might be termed the "chorus line" component of Durkheim's vision of life in a primitive society. But the difference is one of emphasis only; the conventional contemporary view of culture in essence follows Durkheim's assumptions about mechanical solidarity: A collection of persons is a society when they *share* a culture, when they "all adhere to the same set of common beliefs and sentiments." The existence of this shared system explains why the members of the social group are able to act in a manner that creates the phenomenon of "a society." Culture, by defining the limits of the thinkable, orders the activity of each member of the society and thus undergirds a "social order."

In order to understand the genesis and continued vitality of this perspective, it is necessary to outline the history of a long-standing crisis of identity suffered by cultural anthropology: American anthropology has, since the time of Franz Boas, seen itself as both a *descriptive* and a *theoretical* endeavor, and it has proudly offered its notion of culture as relevant to both tasks. As a result, no anthropologist has ever been able to convince his or her fellows that he or she knows just what culture is, because it has had to be a term adapted to two very different tasks.

As George Stocking (1982: 207 and *passim*) has elegantly shown, Franz Boas took the decisive step toward the formulation of the modern idea of culture when he began to think of social coherence as perduring over time through the workings of a "system in place," as the "genius" of a people that selected and transformed social, material, and ideational traits with which it came into contact. This system, culture, was thus both the key to a description of a social group and the actual reason that the group retained a characteristic integrity over time. Although it was not necessarily formulated in these terms by Boas, culture thus came to provide a basis both for ethnography and for social theory; an accurate description of a group would entail an account of their culture, that which in a sense constituted the group.

In this context it is particularly important to note that in Boas's thought the characteristic "genius" that constituted culture worked through the medium of the mind. As Boas (1889) pointed out in his early paper "On Alternating Sounds," the learned system which enables a person to make discriminations in a field of sensory impressions in effect reproduces itself by consistently causing the person to construe new impressions on the basis of the existing parameters in the system. As Boas (p. 50) put it, "a new sensation is apperceived by means of similar sensations that form part of our [already existing] knowledge."

"On Alternating Sounds" brings this insight to bear on a linguistic problem, but the repercussions of this general principle can be traced throughout Boas's thought, and in particular in his developing idea of culture. As Stocking (1982: 159) comments, this article "foreshadows a great deal of modern anthropological thought on 'culture'." The stage was set here for the understanding of culture as a determining force exerted on human behavior, working through the medium of the mind.

The nucleus of the modern conception of culture, then, was present, if incompletely worked out, in Boas's thought. Culture, as that which is characteristic of a people, is the key to a scientific description of their way of life. But at the same time it is the pattern, inscribed into the very perceptions of the culture-bearers, that orders their behavior and accounts, therefore, for the existence of an ordered community, a society.

This duality is a major reason Boas's innovation has had such widely ramifying significance: It facilitated a rapprochement between the anthropological conception of culture and the older humanistic tradition from which the anthropological conception had, by the early years of the twentieth century, diverged. The explicit agenda of the humanistic usage, as Raymond Williams (1983) has shown, was to argue for a sphere of human endeavor that was not subject to the moral rationalism of utilitarianism. For the humanists of the nineteenth century, "culture" was the sphere in which true human value was preserved. Thus, culture was potentially the foundation, for both revolutionaries and reactionaries within the tradition, of an ideal community, a community that avoided the conflict, injustice, and fragmentation that characterized industrializing Europe.

In the humanistic tradition, culture was the blueprint for a community; in the pre-Boasian scientific tradition, whether evolutionist or diffusionist, culture was first of all a descriptive term. To speak of the culture of this people or that was to locate their society in an evolutionary hierarchy or diffusionist scheme. With Boas, and for all practical purposes ever since Boas, "culture" took on *both* these senses. Thus, to take one example, consider Kroeber and Kluckhohn's influential statement (1963: 357) that culture is both "patterns of" and "patterns for" behavior. In contemporary usage, culture is the description of a way of life, and at the same time it is a phenomenon that actually works to order that way of life, a *cause* of the way of life.

This position reflects and perpetuates a fundamental theoretical confusion that in turn sustains "culture as consensus." If culture is a description of something characteristic about a social group, it cannot at the same time be asserted to be causing behavior in the group. Although there may very well be something in a social group that exerts influence over members of the group, something that could be called culture, that culture cannot then be asserted to be the same thing, or even the same sort of thing, as a description of behavior in a group.

Consider an imaginary example. An ethnographer visits a community and notices that different community members say and do similar things. He or she keeps a record of these similar things and, upon returning home, writes them down, calling the result a description of the culture of the community. According to the view I am criticizing, this culture is what influences these people to do what they do. Furthermore, since this culture orchestrates human action in the group, it can be said to be the basis of the social order observed by the ethnographer.

Thus the ethnographer's record of the persons' similar actions and utterances—an account of consensus—has emerged as a force actually working in the group. But the ethnographer's "culture" is a product not only of his or her observations of the group but also of descriptive conventions and his or her imagination as well. It is, as Clifford Geertz (1973: 15) has written, a *fiction*, and it cannot be asserted to be acting directly on the real world in any fashion whatsoever (see also Goodenough 1981: 105; Wallace 1961: 42; Schneider 1968: 6).[5] Pierre Bourdieu (1977: 27) locates the problem precisely when he points out that to assert that a description of social order *causes* that social order is to "reify abstractions, by the fallacy of treating the objects constructed by science, whether 'culture,' 'structure,' or 'modes of production,' as realities endowed with a social efficacy, capable of acting as agents responsible for historical actions or as a power capable of constraining practices...."

Such reification, however, is the inevitable consequence of the position—by now deeply entrenched in American social science—that culture is at once a descriptive and a theoretical term. In this context, it is a further consequence of this confusion that is the ultimate focus of my concern. For, in fact, it is not only reasonable but unavoidable to represent culture as consensus in describing a way of life. Any social description (including this one) must resort to the convention of blurring differences of perspective in order to convey a sense of the traditions, values, and habits in a community. However, it is only the dogma that culture is both patterns for and patterns of behavior that allows one then to assert—or, more often, to assume—that such a description may be applied as a theoretical term that *explains* social order in a group.

That a single term, "culture," can be used for both a *description of* a way of life and the *cause of* that way of life (that is, the reason a social order is perpetuated) is, as has been shown, the result of the peculiar history of the term rather than a well-thought-out theoretical argument. The fact that one can use the same word for two things is no evidence for the equivalency of those things. In fact, "culture," meaning description, cannot be the same thing as "culture," meaning force acting in social life. As a corollary, the fact that it is legitimate to depict culture as consensus for purposes of description does not justify the contention that culture may be assumed to enforce consensus, and thereby constitute social order, in a group.

Here I must pause to respond to the protests of a certain kind of common sense. How, a reader may ask, can anyone doubt that social groups have customs and traditions, passed on from generation to generation, which both order social life and are accessible to observers, who can describe them and call them culture?

One can in fact begin to doubt this seemingly unexceptionable assertion if one considers it carefully. For a custom by itself has no existence apart from a community that lives according to its dictates. And the process we call history is nothing but a relentless and ongoing transformation of customs; some traditions are indeed preserved through countless generations, but they are not therefore impervious to change. It is not custom and tradition that order social life; rather, social life is ordered by an enormously complex interaction between custom and the exigencies of historical situations. That interaction occurs in the medium of human activity, and therefore such activity must find a place in any analysis of social life.

The concept of culture has too often directed the social scientist's attention away from the historical context in which any cultural system is observed, and from the all-important social processes whereby the received way of looking at the world is sustained, adapted, or transformed. In some kinds of endeavors this is a mere quibble; anthropology has produced much magnificent ethnography that is ahistorical but nevertheless enormously insightful. In certain kinds of situations, in other words, a kind of shorthand which assumes a perfect continuity between the received and life as lived from moment to moment may be minimally distorting. For other kinds of endeavors, the assumption that culture may be abstracted from history, and from people's use of that which they receive, is absolutely crippling.

Such an endeavor is the description of a commitment system. In a commitment system, the processes whereby persons manipulate the elements of the system are an essential part of its functioning. Persons in complex societies become committed to systematized outlooks such as a religion (as opposed to simply accepting those outlooks) because they find some such system peculiarly, probably uniquely, meaningful. The fact that some members of the society accept such a system while others do not shows that such meaningfulness cannot be understood as something inherent in the commitment system itself; it is only by turning to the person's *use* of the system that the social efficacy of such a system may eventually be fathomed.

The currently dominant approach to cultural analysis in the United States, which is usually called symbolic anthropology, departs from the assumptions of culture as consensus, and thus rejects this claim. It is, in fact, the system of symbols *itself*, say the various forms of symbolic anthropology, that must be the focus of cultural analysis. In this sense, "semiotic anthropology" might be a more appropriate label for these approaches than is "symbolic anthropology." For, although various schools of symbolic anthropology can be clearly distinguished from one another, most of them are united in endorsing the fundamental assumption that cultural systems are semiotic systems. Cultural systems, in other words, signify; they are systems of signs.

The development of semiotic approaches to cultural systems has occurred as a direct or indirect response to broader currents of twentieth-century thought. Modern analytic philosophy, in particular, has demonstrated the flimsiness of age-old assumptions about the importance of "interior" mental states in language use and in social life as a whole. Concisely put, it has come to look naive to predicate an outlook of human action on the importance of "ideas," something that traditional understandings of culture tended to do. In response to this development, semiotic theories of culture have appeared, views in which the unit of culture is not the idea but the sign, the public representation of the idea.

To oversimplify somewhat, one could say that, while older understandings of culture stressed that culture exerted control over the mind, semiotic approaches have gone one step further and in essence argued that the mind need not be considered in cultural analysis. Thus, the tendency to locate agency in cultural systems, a tendency to which cultural scientists have always been inordinately prone, has been given new impetus by the semiotic view. Modern arguments on meaning have been read—I think it is safe to say misread—as implying that, since the meaning of signs is not a psychological state, it must be a simple function of the sign itself. The result of this is that semiotic approaches have insisted that the meanings of culture may be discerned by an exclusive focus on the cultural system *per se*. The essential mechanism of culture as consensus, the conviction that it is culture rather than persons that constitute society, is thereby clothed in the latest style and paraded out once again.[6]

The result of this position is precisely what one would expect. It has been remarked that culture as consensus construes culture as constituting human action and human social capacities. In semiotic anthropology, culture goes on to constitute the human mind. In the work of Claude Lévi-Strauss, for example, this tendency takes shape in the claim that certain cultural systems are autonomous levels of "objective thought" which may be studied independently of any subject: "I believe that mythology, more than anything else, makes it possible to illustrate such objectified thought and to provide empirical proof of its reality" (Lévi-Strauss 1969: 11).

In Clifford Geertz's work, the same tendency is manifested in a different guise, the assertion that thought may be considered a public activity (1973: 214ff.). "Thinking," he has written (Geertz 1983: 153), "is a matter of the intentional manipulation of cultural forms, and outdoor activities like plowing or peddling are as good examples of it as closet experiences like wishing or regretting." Thus Geertz urges an "ethnographic" approach to thought, wherein the analysis of cultural forms is equated with the interpretation of thought.

I do not contend that these statements are in themselves implausible. One can sympathize with the attempt to escape what Geertz (1973: 362), following Gilbert Ryle, has called the "secret grotto" conception of the human mind. The suggestion that cultural products may be regarded as extrinsic thought, so literally so that the activity molded by culture is the activity of the mind, is potentially a fruitful one. However, such an approach must be supplemented by a well-developed set of instruments for investigating and talking about social and historical processes. To reconstrue mind as culture, one must be able to talk about the kind of flexible adaptation to circumstance that goes on every day (at least to some extent) in any society, for this is an important part of the work of the mind. Such a discussion is conspicuously absent in semiotic approaches because they share the fundamental assumption of "culture as consensus," that culture is a coercive orthodoxy. In fact, it is fair to say that on this issue recent semiotic approaches have advanced not an inch from Durkheim's (1915: 18) dizzying claim: "every mind being drawn into the same eddy, the individual type nearly confounds itself with that of the race."

It is especially in the analysis of a commitment system, then, that conventional approaches to culture—including semiotic ones—prove inadequate. The decisive processes whereby the believer uses the system are never considered in such approaches. Rather, an interpretation offered by the analyst is claimed to be the appropriate focus of study. Depending on the particular approach, this interpretation may or may not be intended to be representative of what believers themselves think. One of the central arguments of this book is that presumably consensual symbols and interpretations are simply not useful topics around which to organize a discussion of a commitment system. In what sense can two believers be said to "share" an element of culture—say, an important religious symbol such as Jesus Christ—if they agree on the importance of the symbol but offer divergent interpretations thereof, and furthermore trace the implications of the symbol for their lives quite differently? In observing and talking to members of Immanuel Church, I found little agreement or discernible consensus on even the fundamental symbols of faith. Of course, most members shared a great deal in terms of their attitudes and beliefs, but I found that it was not possible to specify exactly the boundaries of that sharing. There were always exceptions and subtle shades of difference among the church members.

The point is not to deny that Immanuel Church, like any other functioning social group, is stamped by a "remarkable tacit consensus" (Tylor 1889: 10). To outline the boundaries of that consensus, in a rough sort of way, would certainly convey to the reader a picture of life in this group. But that picture would be an abstraction, and it would contribute little or nothing to the understanding of how the elements of a commitment system actually enter into and affect the lives of believers. In other words, I question whether the existence or appearance of consensus is of importance for understanding how a commitment system may work to hold a social group together and how it works in the lives of actors.

Rather, I will suggest that certain of the processes through which believers at Immanuel Church find meaning in the symbols of their faith may be the most useful starting points in the search for such understanding. These phenomena are not, as most contemporary approaches would assume, processes through which culture users attribute conventional meanings to symbols. They are instead the seizing of cultural resources by believers in order to construct their conceptions of who they are, often on a very basic level. Such symbols are subsequently discovered by believers, usually in emotional moments of profound insight, to express certain important truths about the self and its integration into the social world.

These moments of discovery are apt to be labeled by believers as experiences of grace. The process of appropriation and rediscovery of culture that is so obvious in the experience of grace is a particularly clear example of the level of activity in which a form of culture is used and thereby enters into the lives of actors. By examining such examples in detail, I hope to formulate answers to the two central sociological questions I have emphasized: How do the cultural symbols in this group influence action, and what role do they play in sustaining social cohesion?

In sum, I want to outline a set of principles concerning the operation of culture that is appropriate for the commitment system that was observed at Immanuel Church. The starting point for these principles is in itself not new at all; it is the realization that social cohesion, a sense of community, may be generated in processes that have nothing to do with cultural sharing. As is affirmed by a tradition of work on ritual stretching back to Robertson Smith and Durkheim, community may be constituted and strengthened in ritual and ritualized social processes that are better understood as effervescent experiences than as exchanges of meaning.[7]

In Immanuel Church those experiences are construed as moments of grace. In order to avoid the religious implications of "grace," I will use a more neutral word for the relationship between the symbol and the person, "commitment." This term is best introduced by contrasting it to yet another, "belief."[8] To some propositions one assents, one believes. Other propositions are more important, one has an emotional investment in them, they are the certainties that anchor one's world view. To these latter propositions one is *committed*.

Commitment to a proposition or a symbol of any kind entails a relationship between symbol and person that transcends language. Commitment is both more and less than a semantic process, for the symbol to which one is committed does not only represent. In the relation of commitment, the symbol blends with experience; it is more likely to appear as a feeling that can be described than as a content that can be deciphered. It is a relation of meaningfulness, not only of meaning.

As will be amply demonstrated, the blending of symbol with experience means that the symbol takes on the features of the self. One feels a relation to the symbol that is so close that a threat to the symbol is likely to be felt as a threat to the self. This kind of relation is, among other things, a strong basis for community. For if you and I are committed to the same thing, we share an almost physical bond, we are united in a part of our very selves. One of the central points of this book is that people may share commitments without sharing beliefs; it follows that they may constitute a community without that community being based in consensus.

The second theoretical issue that must be faced in any attempt to reconstrue culture as commitment is the question "If cultural forms are not assumed to assert direct influence over actors through their meanings, how then *do* they exert influence in social life?" In later chapters I will defend the idea that cultural influence works not, as has often been assumed, through the mind alone but through the body as well. Commitment, I will argue, is an actual *physical* appropriation of cultural forms. The implication of this argument is that culture is a force more deeply established in human activity, but at the same time less coercive, than has usually been assumed. Cultural influence, I will hold, manifests itself in characteristic dispositions, postures, habits, in short in the patterns that characterize an actor's experience and enable the actor to formulate himself or herself as a self.[9] In such a view, the patterning of social life occurs because men and women with characteristic dispositions are constantly creating and reproducing those patterns, not because the pattern has a reality that imposes itself somehow in social life.[10]

It will be noted that such an approach roots social processes at the level of the person, and it may be further asserted that such a tactic reflects the individualistic presuppositions of the author or of the men and women at Immanuel Church. The former comment is valid, the latter is not. It is indeed my intent to concentrate on and draw attention to social processes, operating through the level of the person, that order social life. Such an approach, however, is by no means incompatible with the position that social patterns may be located in institutions, in ideologies, or in other social formations. My point is simply that the isolation of such patterns is not the end of a social analysis; rather, it is a prelude to the important question, how do these patterns penetrate into the lives of actors? Such a question is motivated not by individualism but by concern for the integrity of the persons who are the ultimate focus of any social analysis. It is not being trapped by an ideology of individualism to point out that human life *never* proceeds along the lines of Durkheim's stereotyped movements, that men and women always utilize their cultural legacy in a manner that is at least somewhat adaptive, flexible, and even creative.

It is to the neglected processes of cultural use, of how cultural forms function in the lives of persons, that I will turn in the following chapters. My rejection of "culture as consensus" should be seen as a dissatisfaction with current ideas about how culture works, and not as a denial that the men and women of Immanuel Church share—at least in a loose sense of that word—conceptions, meanings, and articulable values. I will in fact devote most of the following two chapters to a description of a shared heritage, the history and characteristics of this church. Such information is necessary background to the description of "culture as commitment" that follows. I insist, however, that such description does not in itself take us very far in understanding the relationship between a cultural system and social order. That relationship, particularly if the cultural system in question is a commitment system, can be studied only by turning to the processes whereby believers use the elements of their faith. The following analysis is devoted to an exploration of those processes and their implications.

2

The Pietist Heritage

In the chapters to follow, much variation will be demonstrated in the Christian beliefs held by members of Immanuel Church. It is my conviction that this variation is in itself important, worthy of notice, and that it must not be reduced to homogeneity, as culture so often is in anthropological acounts. This is not to deny, of course, that many beliefs are shared at Immanuel Church; above all, believers there use a common religious language and elaborate on a common religious heritage. In this chapter I will examine the historical derivation of that heritage.

Svenska Missionsförbundet (The Swedish Mission Covenant, hereafter SMF)—the denomination of which Immanuel Church is a part—was formed by secession from the Swedish state church in 1879. The story told here, however, must begin earlier. The formation of SMF was the culmination of a process initiated early in the eighteenth century, when a wave of religious awakening that had appeared throughout northern Europe in the previous century began to penetrate into Sweden. The new religious outlook was called Pietism, a label first applied by enemies of the movement but eventually adopted by the participants themselves (Meyer 1984: 5–6). Although Pietism is little studied in America, it was a movement with extraordinarily wide-ranging influence in European spiritual and intellectual history. Neither the enlightenment nor romanticism—to say nothing of European religious history during the last three centuries—can be rightly understood without an appreciation of the part the Pietist spirit played in these developments. It is appropriate, then, to spend some time getting to know this remarkable movement.

Historians are agreed that Pietism was a reform movement within Protestantism that took shape during the seventeenth century. They are not agreed on how to draw the boundaries of the movement. Some adhere to a restricted usage whereby Pietism is confined to a late seventeenth-century attempt to reform German Lutheranism, while others hold that a much broader range of religious groups, including parts of English Puritanism, are appropriately labeled Pietist (Stoeffler 1965: 8). Here I will follow the spirit of the latter strategy, which is based in

> the conviction that all experiential Protestantism during the post-Reformation period can be treated as an essential unity. It constitutes a movement which, if seen in its full range, penetrated all of Protestantism during the seventeenth and eighteenth centuries and the influence of which has been felt wherever Protestantism has appeared. (Stoeffler 1965: 8)

By the term "experiential," Stoeffler intends to refer to a faith that stresses not the adherence to doctrine but a personal experience of the power of God as the foundation of faith. This experiential tradition, rooted in the seventeenth and eighteenth centuries, is what I mean by the term Pietism.

As will be shown below, SMF is derived from a tradition of piety within Swedish Lutheranism which had been influenced by a wide range of Christian outlooks, including British and American Evangelical Christianity and early German Pietism. It would not be possible to trace these influences genetically. What can be done is to demonstrate a fundamental theological affinity between SMF and the experiential tradition that Stoeffler labels Pietism, and this will be my goal here.

Fundamental to the Pietist outlook is a distinction between "inner" and "external" Christianity.[1] In order to understand this distinction it is necessary to realize that the Protestant orthodoxies which Pietist movements reacted against had, by the seventeenth century, developed into excessively rigid styles of religious life. The Pietists complained that too much religious concern was being directed toward sterile debates over dogma, that overly literal interpretations of "salvation by grace through faith" had led to a de-emphasis on the righteous life, and that too many Christians practiced a faith limited to the prescribed observances and sacraments.

In opposition to this externality, the Pietist stressed the supreme importance of, in Stoeffler's (1965: 13 – 14) words, "the personally meaningful relationship of the individual to God." He goes on: "The terms characteristic of the Pietistic tradition such as 'experiential,' 'inward,' or 'personal,' always have reference to this fact."

This distinction between inner and outer Christianity reflects the dichotomy, drawn in the previous chapter, between commitment and belief. All of us are familiar, from our own experience, with the distinction between that which one believes uncritically and that which one believes *in*.[2] And we recognize that the difference is, in part at least, one of emotion. That to which one is committed, that which one believes in, has an important emotional valence. Surely this is in part what the term "inner relationship" refers to, even among the Pietists, for they shared our habit of thinking of the emotions as within, from the insides. Thus, in part, an inner relationship is one that can be *felt*, a relationship with an emotional component.

Thus, the importance of feeling to a viable Christian faith was emphasized in all branches of Pietism. In the more radical parts of the movement, this emphasis could take on a frankly sensual aspect. The Pietist von Zinzendorf wrote that in proper faith "the heart must burn" (cited in Pinson 1934: 44), and Gottfried Arnold expressed the opinion, lying on his deathbed, that he ate God in every bite of bread (Pinson 1934: 49). Although more sober Pietist elements avoided frank sensuality, they relied heavily on terms like "the heart," "feeling," and "enthusiasm." All agreed with the early Pietist Johann Arndt, who wrote that the true faith is "a feeling, sensation and actual conviction of... God's grace, solace and power" (Pinson 1934: 41).

Another designation for the "inner" relationship is "personal." A faith described by this term must be not only emotional but somehow adapted to the uniqueness of the self. That is, it is only possible to speak of a "personal relationship" in the context of a self that *is* unique, that is sharply delineated from other selves. A relationship is personal if it is based in that uniqueness somehow; it remains impersonal if the self enters into the relationship only on the basis of its general qualities.

From this one can see that, from the believer's perspective, a personal relation between believer and the symbols of faith must be felt to touch something valuable, unique, and characteristic in the self. This entails a mode of interpretation of the symbols of faith that is utterly opposed to the authority of orthodoxy. Orthodoxy, in defining faith strictly, does not build a bridge between the uniqueness of the self and the symbol of faith. The Pietists, by contrast, practiced an alternative form of interpretation, in which the salient meaning of the symbol is ultimately left up to the individual believer (guided always by the Holy Spirit; more on this later). Thus, the Pietists saw Biblical text as having veiled and multiple meanings:

> Pietist commentators were not nearly so completely wedded to the grammatical sense of Biblical texts as their more orthodox and scholastically minded counterparts. While they affirmed a literal grammatical reading they also sought to transcend it. (Frei 1974: 38)

In this way the stress on an "inner" relationship of faith comes to be associated with a stress on inner meanings of scripture. Thus, the late seventeenth-century German Pietist August Francke wrote a work entitled *Christ, the Kernel of the Holy Scriptures,* in which he stressed that God's "meaning is richer than any sea, and his word is deeper than any abyss"[3] (cited in Meyer 1984: 20).

The metaphor of "innerness" can also be linked to the typical organizational form of Pietism. In the German branch of the movement, which produced the earliest and most significant effects in Sweden, Pietist groups took the form of conventicles, which were collections of the faithful *within* the organized church. Again, the structural purpose of this innovation was to provide a flexible mediator between the individual believer and the church hierarchy. Conventicles met to discuss the Bible and its application in the task of constructing a pious life. "They were," writes Stoeffler (1965: 237) of the conventicles, "meant to constitute one of the major facets of the new reformation. Through them, pastors and dedicated laymen were intended to work in concert to add to the reformation of doctrine the reformation of life."

This concern with the righteous life was another important feature of Pietism. As is well known, Luther's central innovation in instigating the German reformation was the contention that it is *not* through good works or the efficacy of the sacraments that the believer is saved but rather through God's grace, offered to and received by the person with faith. This does not mean that Luther held that good works were an unnecessary part of Christian practice. His point was rather that good works were the *result* rather than the *cause* of the reception of grace. He wrote:

> Plainly faith is enough for the Christian man. He has no need for works to be made just....But he is not therefore to be lazy or loose. Good works do not make a man good, but a good man does good works. (cited in Bainton 1956: 111–12)

In the Protestant orthodoxy against which Pietism rose, the first part of this statement was stressed at the expense of the second (Stoeffler 1965: 11). Spener and other Pietists argued strongly against such a position, claiming that to be true to Luther's intent one must emphasize the importance of truly Christian conduct. Stoeffler (1962: 241) has commented:

> Spener believed uncompromisingly that Christ came not only to justify men but to sanctify them as well.... The individual must respond to God's grace and bend his will toward the continuous amendment of life. Spener regarded as one of the major errors of his day the habit of contemporary Lutheran theologians to disregard God's rightful claim to a holy life.

The reader will recognize in most of these features the basis of a radical individualism. In the first place, the salient aspect of Christianity here is the relationship between the individual and God. Furthermore, that relationship is depicted in various ways as perfectly adapted to the "inner" uniqueness of the individual. Emotionally, intellectually, even organizationally, man's connection to God manifested itself, according to the Pietists, as a relationship between individual and God. True religion was considered to issue in a *personally* meaningful faith and the *person's* Christian conduct. Yet it would be a fundamental error to conclude that Pietism represented an individualistic trend in the way that term is generally understood today.

The conventional understanding of individualism is formulated as a contrast to, in Louis Dumont's (1965: 14) term, holism. Individualism labels a situation in which the individual is valued over the social whole; holism refers to a situation in which the value of the social whole is paramount. The person in an individualistic society, Dumont goes on to say, is conceived as an "independent, autonomous and thus (essentially) non-social moral being" (Dumont 1965: 15).

To associate Pietism with individualism in this form would be to utterly misconceive the nature of that movement. For the stress on good works in Pietism—the stress, one could say, on an awareness of society—is an expression of a deeper and vital impulse. The radically individualist Pietist von Zinzendorf, associated with the Moravians, expressed this impulse when he wrote: "God has created us for *Gemeinschaft*" (community) and, "without *Gemeinschaft* there is no Christianity" (cited in Pinson 1934: 68).

The conviction that God enters into a personal relationship with each individual believer entails the possibility that the believers are all united in God. Thus, the fundamental point that must be grasped regarding the individual and community in Pietism is not that the individual is more highly valued than community but, rather, that the individual is in a logical and theological sense *prior to* community, which is also highly valued. Community is *derived* from the relationship between individual and God, which remains basic. To quote von Zinzindorf again: "The community of Christendom on earth is based on the principle that every soul knows in whom it believes. Only out of the personal experience is *communion*, the community of the holy, created" (cited in Pinson 1934: 67).

The logical priority of the relation between individual and God here does not entail any devaluation of the importance of community, as is characteristic of the "individualism" described by Dumont. Further evidence of the recognition of the importance of community in Pietism can be found in its hermeneutics, its theory of biblical interpretation.[4] For, although the Pietists saw interpretation as an act of the individual, they also held that the believer is guided in that act by the group as a whole. One application of this principle can be observed in the conventicles, which were groups for reading and discussing the Bible. More basic was the theological principle, most fully developed in the German Pietist Oetinger, that it was through the representation of the group within the individual—what he called the *sensus communis*—that the Word is properly interpreted. In fact, Oetinger held that not only scriptural but *all* truth was apprehended through the functioning of the *sensus communis*. This position was formulated in opposition to rationalism. Reason, as a *human* capacity, is vulnerable to error, but the *sensus communis* "always operates with God" (Gadamer 1975: 27).

In sum, Pietism is an individualistic tendency in that it posits the relationship between the individual and God as fundamental. Unlike Catholicism, which conceives the connection between person and God as mediated by the church, Pietism sees the relationship between person and God as the *basis* of the church. This individualism, however, must not be understood as a disregard for the value of community, for in fact Pietism stressed the importance of community in various ways. (None of this, of course, is to deny that the logic of the Pietist type of individualism tends, over time, to militate against the values of community.)

Two final characteristics of Pietism that I wish to note here, without further discussion at this time, are the stress on the personal conversion experience and the concern with evangelism and mission work. Francke wrote that the *Wiedergeburt* (born again) experience of regeneration and commitment to Christianity was essential for all believers (Pinson 1934: 45). Also of great importance, most Pietists felt, was the talk of bringing *others* to Christ, and it is from this Pietist impulse that the Protestant missionary movement arose.

Pietist conventicles, in the form of small groups of "saved" Christians that met in private homes and were often led by laymen, began to appear in Sweden around 1700 (Gustafsson 1968: 117, 119).[5] Sweden had a powerful state church with a Lutheran theology, and this threat to the authority of the state church was put down in 1726 by a law which made these gatherings illegal. However, the church also tried to satisfy the growing interest in this type of worship by encouraging its priests to lead home meetings, according, of course, to official theological doctrines (Wennås 1978: 29).

In spite of the new law, the conventicles continued, led often by priests who had themselves undergone conversions and were sympathetic to the Pietist outlook (Wennås 1978: 29). The groups that sprang up over the following decades came to be known as *läsare*, "the readers," because of their stress upon reading the Bible as a method of returning to a purer religion.

Pietism also traveled to Great Britain and America, where it was eventually transformed into the strong evangelical traditions of those countries. Evangelicalism was subsequently a substantial influence on Swedish dissenting religious groups in its own right, as evangelical groups branched out from Great Britain into Sweden during the nineteenth century. The main characteristics of these movements were an emphasis on personal faith and conversion, on the Bible as the ultimate spiritual authority, and on an expansive social concern expressed at home in the stress on reform and/or revivalism, and abroad in mission work.

Groups of *läsare* persisted throughout the eighteenth century, and in the nineteenth century their role as the organizational center of Swedish dissent was supplemented by the appearance of Methodist and Baptist groups. In 1842 Carl Olof Rosenius, the son of a priest associated with the radical *läsare* groups of northern Sweden, cofounded a magazine called *The Pietist* (*Pietisten*) that soon became one of Sweden's most widely read publications (Wennås 1978: 31).

In 1856 the growing "new evangelical" movement attained the status of an officially recognized institution within the state church. An organization called *Evangeliska Fosterlandsstiftelsen* (The National Evangelical Organization, EFS) was formed to coordinate various activities of the revival movement. To some extent EFS was intended to counter ever-increasing separatist pressure, especially from the Baptists and Methodists, which would have led to the secession from the state church of its "new evangelical" parts.

This organizational strategy to preserve the integrity of the state church temporarily papered over the differences between orthodoxy and Pietist dissent, but it did nothing to resolve underlying differences. The basis of those differences can be simply summarized by stating that EFS members saw themselves as "saved," as having attained a personal, inner relationship to Christ through a conversion experience. Furthermore, they held that such a relationship was the essence of a valid Christian faith.

As an institution within the state church, EFS's activities should have been merely a supplement to those of the parent organization. The sacraments, for instance, were to be administered by the state church. The position that a Christian was one who had been "saved," however, exerted a constant strain on this position. Should the true Christian partake in a communion ceremony that he or she knew included state church members who were not true believers? How could such a ceremony be genuine? Of what use was state church ordination if it was the personal decision for Christ that was determinative of the true Christian?

At base these questions came down to the issue of whether the established church or the saved individual (and collections thereof) was the channel of divine grace. Walan (1978: 13) has characterized this underlying issue as the "concept of church" (*församlingssyn*):

> Ever since the founding of EFS, the question of the concept of church had been a problem for the "new evangelical" movement. It had appeared in various guises down through the years, and sometimes the connection to the problem of church concept had not been obvious to individual members of the movement. From a superficial perspective, the problems were concerned with other things, for example, commu-

nion, calling, lay preaching or the doctrine of atonement. But at bottom was the question of what was meant by Christ's church.

As a result, the local organizations of which EFS was composed were subjected to a constant tension between their official (supplementary) purpose and their ideologically induced tendencies to take over functions from the state church. A word on the nature of these local organizations is in order. Often starting out as associations organized for a particular end, such as the founding of an orphanage, these groups were retained after the realization of their goals in order to further the work of evangelization. Thus, although the nature of the organizations varied, they were assumed under the general functional rubric of "mission (or evangelization) associations" (missionsföreningar).

The tensions working on the mission associations were aggravated after 1868 by the radical theological doctrines of P. P. Waldenström, who had assumed the editorship of *The Pietist*. Although not himself a committed separatist, Waldenström formulated the uncompromising theological positions on atonement and communion that came to divide EFS into two opposing camps in the following years. It is not necessary to discuss these theological doctrines in any detail here; suffice it to say that Waldenström's positions arose ultimately from a strict application of the Pietist sense of the church as the association of true believers in an area. Those who followed Waldenström were unwilling to compromise what they saw as their pure principles when these came into conflict with the state church. Other members of EFS, on the other hand, stressed the importance of the bond with the church and the need for compromise.

In this situation, a splintering of EFS was inevitable, and it came during the summer of 1878, when a group of Waldenström's followers formed SMF. Interestingly, Waldenström himself regarded the separation as a necessary evil and seems to have retained the hope of a reunification of SMF and EFS until his death in 1917 (Wennås 1978: 45). He was firmly set against the development of SMF into a denomination, for he regarded the very idea of a denomination as unbiblical. In the New Testament, he said, one finds independent, free-standing congregations; modern religious bodies should be organized after this pattern (Wennås 1978: 44 – 45; Andersson 1934: 160).

So, although there were those who pressed for a strong central organization coordinating member congregations (i.e., a denomination) from the earliest years of SMF, Waldenström used all his influence to combat this view. SMF was therefore originally conceived not as a church (a label claimed by the state church), nor as a denomination, but as a coordinating organ for the various evangelization activities of the affiliated but independent congregations.

In this context, the selection of the name *Svenska Missionsförbundet*— The Swedish Mission Covenant—becomes comprehensible: the new organi-

zation was not a church but a loose federation of the free-standing congregations and "mission associations" that had withdrawn from EFS in 1878 and
the succeeding years.[6] At this time, SMF seems to have seen itself according
to the congregationalist pattern, as a decentralized organizational form
granting considerable autonomy to individual congregations. In 1890, the
general conference of the church dispatched the following message to the
Congregationalists in America:

> There are many national differences between us, differences that prevent
> a formal union, but we rejoice in our spirit to know that you work in
> accord with, on the whole, the same Christian principles as we, so that
> we go along the same path and so that you hope to be among Americans
> what we are among the Swedes. (Andersson 1934: 158)

However, as SMF grew from 80 affiliated congregations in 1880 to 1,102
in 1903 (Wennås 1978: 42), the need for a stronger central organization
became ever more obvious. There was also sentiment for a denomination
among some elements of the church leadership. Waldenström fought these
tendencies by the sheer force of his personality until his death, but after 1917
the central organization began to move steadily in the direction of denom-
inationalism. The extent of this shift can perhaps be best observed in the following editorial which appeared in SMF's official newspaper in 1977:

> SMF—Change Your Name on Your 100th Birthday!
> Wouldn't it be appropriate to celebrate our denomination's 100th birth-
> day with a change of name, from *Svenska Missionsförbundet* to some-
> thing more manageable and contemporary? A name which proclaims
> what our congregational and denominational life stands for nowadays.
> A name that is easier to handle in contact with our nation's eight million
> inhabitants.... (*Svensk Veckotidning,* June 24, 1977; cited in Wennås
> 1978: 251)

The author goes on to suggest a number of new names, all of which
include the word *kyrka* (church): *Förbundskyrkan* (The Covenant Church),
Sveriges Evangeliska Kyrka (Sweden's Evangelical Church), and
Framtidskyrkan (The Church of the Future). In addition to the benefits of
manageability and a modern ring, the author is also arguing for the need to
express a change in the movement's sociological status, namely that, on the
organizational level, SMF has become a church, a centralized and bureau-
cratized religious institution.[7]
The name has not changed, however, and its persistence hints that, in a
sense, the transformation to a church has not taken place on the ideological
level. The old conception of the congregation endures side by side with a
well-developed bureaucracy. This persistence has both ideological and organizational manifestations; a single congregation like Immanuel Church still
has considerable independence in SMF. More important in this context is the

fact that the congregationalist format has served to reinforce and preserve certain of the old Pietist principles associated with its stance in opposition to an established church form. For example, there is a de-emphasis in congregationalist churches on the organized clergy and an absence of creedal structure. Although SMF has trained ministers for its congregations since its inception, a high level of lay participation in church life has always characterized the organization. This has been a particular advantage since the turn of the century, for not only has SMF escaped the full wrath of revolutionary and reformist anticlericalism, but the constant input from life outside the church has proved adaptive in a time when so many Christian churches seemed to be drifting away from relevance. [8]

Furthermore, since there is not as much stress in congregationalist churches on the institutional apparatus of the church—ministry, sacraments, and creed—as mediators between heaven and earth, greater weight falls on scripture-reading and on the congregation itself to fulfill this role. It has been mentioned that the early Swedish Pietists, the *läsare,* placed great stress on reading the Bible, and the this activity continues to be regarded as vital in SMF today. The latter of these mediating devices, the congregation, is no less important in SMF. In this church, as among congregationalists in general, there is a sense in which the very sociality, the fellowship in the congregation, is believed to be a basis for a true and proper understanding of God's will (Meagher, O'Brien, and Aherne 1979: 877). Such a belief, again, preserves a central element of SMF's Pietist heritage, the appreciation of the role of the group in the formation and application of Christian faith. This principle will emerge as one of the fundamental themes of this book.

The influence of the congregationalist pattern is not the only organizational feature of the church that has functioned to maintain the ideological principles of the Pietists. The unresolved ambiguity between SMF as church and as a federation of evangelical organizations has entailed a strong continuing sense of the social goals of the movement—the goals, that is, that originally defined the *missionsföreningar.* Thus, although SMF has always been an organization of believers, what they have been organized for has never been defined in strictly spiritual terms. Particularly during its first twenty-five years, SMF was conceived by many as a "supplement" to the state church, the main task of which was the furtherance of *väckelse,* awakening or revival.

SMF has remained suspended between its strictly spiritual goals and its utopian aims of social reconstruction. *Väckelse* included temperance work as well as revival meetings, foreign missionary activity but also hospitals and schools. Given this tension between communitarian and individualist spiritual motives, it is hardly surprising that the question "to what extent does the Christian faith entail social involvement?" has been a topic of debate since the earliest years of the movement. The following quotation from a pamphlet published in 1914 provides evidence of a controversy at that time between those who sought an emotional spiritual awakening and those who conceived the church's task more in terms of social responsibility:

> You brothers, who sometimes complain about the fact that it is not so "hot at the meetings" (*varmt på mötena*) or that there isn't the same spiritual power in our congregations as in your younger years and your first time with God, listen now: return to your first faith and your first deeds in order to once again receive your earlier power and joy. Do not collect riches on earth lest ye lose your salvation and condemn your children, but rather use those riches for the welfare of humanity and to bring the kingdom of God. (Andersson 1914: 10)

The same theme, the debate over the spiritual and social content of *väckelse*, SMF's continuing goal, can be found in the writings of any decade of this century. It is interesting that the invariable vehicle for this debate is historical narrative: one proves one's point about what SMF should be doing now by pointing to what the movement did in its early years. The unstated assumption is evidently that the formative years of the movement provide a clue as to its essence.

The following exchange, which occurred in the church newspaper in 1971, is a good example. First BZ writes that the reason SMF stopped expanding in the middle 1920s can be traced to the introduction at that time of an American style evangelism into SMF, which differed from the Swedish type in being "sectarian" and in discouraging social responsibility. The adoption of this form, says BZ, made SMF a "foreign movement not in tune with the socially conscious spirit of the age" and was thus largely responsible for its subsequent decline.

In reply, WO writes:

> The depiction of our 19th century forefathers' interest in social matters is too schematic and convenient.[9] It ignores the strong Pietist tendency present at that time. Avoidance of the things of this world was stressed in a manner that is difficult to reconcile with today's demands for openness.... There were... reservations about engaging in organized groups which were construed as a threat against the congregation. There were warnings as well about politics. They feared the possibility of the spirit being secularized (*förvärldsligad*). (cited in Wennås 1978: 210)

What these men are arguing about is the question of whether SMF is above all a spiritual institution for the rescue of individual souls or whether it is in essence a religiously toned social movement for the improvement of society. The persistence of this argument over the last century, of course, proves that both are fundamentally true. SMF is a religious movement

grounded in a radical individualism, but it has also been a popular movement that has consistently highlighted an emphasis on persons as social crea-
tures with an obligation to engage in the reconstruction of the society
around them.

In many ways, then, SMF is tightly linked to its Pietist past. The organizational pecularities of the movement, as well as the fact that it continues to
coexist with a powerful state church, have prevented SMF from progressing
along an expected path of institutionalization. As a result, the congregations
in SMF have retained something of the organizational flavor of the original
Pietist conventicles, and with that organization an ideology has likewise been
preserved.

The core of that ideology can be read in the theology of the *sensus
communis,* an archaic and fragile conception that expresses something that
seems to have been lost in many other quarters of modern life. In this notion
a sense of moral individualism, a belief that the individual is an autonomous
center of responsibility, is welded to an appreciation of the social basis of
knowledge and indeed of human life as a whole. The *sensus communis* looks
for God in a piety that would combine moral individualism with the sense of
the community and make them one.

It is my contention in this study that variations on this theme are the
dominant motif in the religious life at Immanuel Church. Members and
leaders in this church struggle to express and remember a truth about their
lives that seems to run counter to much of what they observe and experience
as members of a modern society. There are moments of transcendence,[10]
moments of grace, when some symbol of faith becomes real, when what one
has hoped for and trusted in merges with experience. In such a moment,
believers feel a sense of affirmation of their own existence—they experience
something meaningful about their lives—at the same time that they recognize the profundity of their communal symbols. It is therefore possible, at
least at times, for these men and women to experience a reconciliation that is
all too rare in the modern world, a reconciliation between their individuality
and their sociality.

3

⟨∿⟩

Immanuel Church

In this chapter I will introduce
Immanuel Church to the reader, first by sketching a picture of the church as I
encountered it in the late 1970s and then by looking in some detail at a single
church service that I witnessed during the time I studied the church.
Especially in the latter half of the chapter, I will be working to some extent at
cross purposes to my stated theoretical goals in this work as a whole, and this
deserves some comment. I mean that I will describe, and briefly interpret,
certain enigmatic speeches which constituted a part of the service in question, although I stated earlier that the religious language at Immanuel
Church is best investigated by asking believers what it means to *them*.

This apparent contradiction arises from the fact that in this chapter my
goals are ethnographic. I want to give the reader a sense of what it is like at
Immanuel Church, to describe the building, the church members, the worship service, and so on. Although my interest in the book as a whole centers
on the problem of discussing how individual believers use the symbols of
their faith, in this chapter I have a different goal, and thus I will use different
methods. To discuss a sermon or a hymn, to place it in its social and
historical context, is to say little of what individual believers may make of
that sermon or hymn. Nevertheless, the descriptive task is in itself important, if only to give the reader a sense of the background against which
individual interpretations take shape.

To the observer unfamiliar with the Swedish religious scene, the first thing to note about SMF in general, and Immanuel Church in particular, is that it is what is called a *frikyrka*, a free church. This simply means that SMF is not the official state church, into which all Swedes are born (membership in the state church comes with citizenship) and some 95 percent of them remain.[1] In fact, many members of Immanuel Church have never officially withdrawn from the state church; they retain their membership in the state church while practicing their faith in SMF.

The fact that membership in the state church is automatic, while one must decide to join SMF, creates some predictable differences between the groups. Taken as a whole, the state church is legendarily moribund (which is not to say that there are not vital churches and active Christians within it). Of the 95 percent of the populace who belong to the state church, only about 3 percent will be in church on any given Sunday.[2] That there is more vitality in SMF, more participation among the membership, can be seen in the statistic that the percentage of SMF members who report attending church *at least* once a week is 67 percent.[3]

My perception of the vitality in this denomination was further augmented by the congregation I chose to study, which is by all accounts a lively and successful one. Immanuel Church, located in downtown Stockholm, has about 1,300 members and is regarded as the national cathedral of SMF. It should be noted that this book is a study of Immanuel Church, and not of SMF as a whole, for the simple reason that the author attended the church, not the denomination. On the other hand, most of the written and historical sources on which this study is based apply to SMF as a whole, and substantial parts of what I will say here has relevance to the entire denomination.

The reader may nevertheless still wonder, how representative is the congregation I will discuss here of the denomination as a whole? This question is somewhat difficult to answer. Immanuel Church is certainly larger than the average church in SMF, it is likely that its congregation is more diverse and liberal, and it is also a safe guess that this congregation employs some of the more talented ministers in SMF. In at least one sense, Immanuel Church is surely atypical; the highest proportion of SMF members to population has always been in southern Sweden where, by all reports, a more conservative and morally strict religion is practiced than that which I observed in downtown Stockholm at Immanuel Church.

These qualifications are not trivial, but in the end it must be granted that the features of church life in Immanuel Church which I discuss here probably hold in their general outlines, as well as in some of their particulars, for SMF as a whole. As was noted in the previous chapter, SMF has a strong tradition of congregational independence, and therefore to argue that the denomination can be boiled down to *any* individual congregation is apt to be misleading. But Immanuel Church, with its high status in the denomination and its constant influx of SMF members from all corners of Sweden, holds a reasonable claim to being the most representative, if not the most typical, congregation in SMF.

How representative, then, is Immanuel Church of other Swedish denominations, in particular, of the state church? A careful answer to this question, of course, would be an apt topic for another book. Here it is sufficient to say that SMF is an offshoot of the state church and has existed since the time of the split in close interaction with that church; both have been subject to the same range of social forces. At the same time, as has been explained, SMF has tenaciously preserved a good deal of its Pietist heritage. These elements could perhaps be found in some state church congregations but are certainly not typical in that group. In the conclusion, I will argue that the ideas about grace that I observed at Immanuel Church may in some sense be widely diffused throughout Swedish society, in secular as well as religious institutions. Such a position further complicates the question of comparison between religious bodies, and for the most part I will not address this question here.

If a visitor were to walk into Immanuel Church for the first time on a Sunday morning, as I did in the late summer of 1978, the first things to catch his or her attention would probably be the form of the worship service, the church building itself, and the people in the congregation. If the visitor were an American familiar with the form of worship in mainstream American Protestant churches, he or she would probably be struck, below the level of the strange language and the slight unfamiliarities, by a basic feeling of comfort and recognition. The Sunday morning service at Immanuel Church is, in its broad outlines and tone of feeling, not much different from the services at mainstream Protestant churches in America, or at the state church in Sweden.

Of course, if one were to do a careful comparison, important differences would emerge. For example, SMF lacks a creed, and in general the atmosphere is less "high church"—less dependent on formal, ritualized elements—than at, say, the Swedish state church. There is also a high proportion of lay participation in the church service. Lay members of the church, for example, often participate in worship services by reading from the Bible, giving speeches, or singing. At the same time, this variation in the normal format of the worship service is a very well-controlled process. As one woman who is quoted at length in a later chapter notes, it is only the most talented and dependable church members who are asked to serve in these capacities. I once heard an elderly woman in a front pew attempt to add something, spontaneously, to a brief speech by a pastor. The somewhat disconcerted minister ignored her, and, after an instant of acute embarrassment, the service proceeded as if nothing had happened. It is possible that some spontaneous contributions might be better received than this one was

(I did not hear what the woman said; it may have been antagonistic or otherwise inappropriate). But in general, the worship service at Immanuel Church is a far cry from, say, the participatory form that characterizes Pentecostal groups.

Normally, the Sunday morning worship service begins with a ringing of the church bells and an organ prelude. Next, one or two hymns are sung, interspersed with short prayers or Bible passages read from the front of the church. Then comes an introduction to the service by one of the pastors. Such a speech may contain a reference to the date in the church calendar, the themes for the coming service, a greeting to special visitors, or a short meditation on some recent event. After this, usually a solo or a choir anthem precedes a reading from the scriptures, after which yet another hymn is sung. Then comes a sermon, fifteen to twenty minutes long, based on a New Testament text. In general, I was impressed by these sermons, which I found sophisticated and compelling, but church members I talked with sometimes seemed more cynical than I. I heard many complaints that the sermons were boring or distant; some people noted that they had "heard it all before."

After the sermon, this musical congregation invariably joins in another hymn, during which the offering is taken. The offering is followed by a prayer having to do with the money just collected, and then by announcements. Another anthem or solo may follow, but inevitably there is a long prayer which ends with the congregation repeating the Lord's Prayer together. The service closes with a final hymn and a short blessing, followed by a respectful silence. Then the organ breaks in, beginning a postlude that signals that it is time for listeners to gather up their belongings and file out of the church.

The Sunday morning service is the main focus of church life, but other kinds of activities go on throughout the week. Worship services, usually more informal and often organized around a guest speaker, are also held on Sunday, Wednesday, and Friday evenings. These services, in my experience, are usually well attended. In addition, interest and youth groups, study circles and special events are held throughout the week.

Since I regularly attended two of these study circles and the meetings of the church youth group while I was in Sweden, I can also convey some idea of the structure of these groups. A study circle is simply a group of men and women, of a convenient size for discussion (say, under fifteen persons), which is organized around—and meets regularly to discuss—some particular topic of interest. It is difficult to convey to the reader who is unfamiliar with Sweden how much of that nation's intellectual and social life is implicated in the workings of study circles. Each year, nearly two million adults—between a quarter and a third of the adult population of Sweden—participate in study circles offered by a wide range of groups, from labor unions to universities.

The first study circle I began to attend was formed around a group of well-established church members (all over thirty and several beyond retirement age) which met to discuss *samlevnadsfrågor*, questions having to do with what we might call personal life (although the Swedish formulation, which means literally "questions concerning living in common," lacks some of the individualistic flavor of the American phrase). The group was led by a woman, in her late fifties, of substantial authority and a rather compelling personality. She was a strong and, I felt, remarkable woman. She led our group in a series of discussions on topics (such as sex) that would have made most members uncomfortable had it not been for her substantial openness and grace.

The second study circle in which I became involved was a more variable group with somewhat younger members (although this group too had a few participants in their 50s and 60s). The meetings of this group were usually devoted to international politics. For instance, we held a ten-week class on the problem of world peace: the arms race, the causes of war, and so on.

To describe a typical member at Immanuel Church is probably not possible, nor would it be desirable.[4] For one of the most striking features of this church is the diversity of its membership: both active communist party members and Bible-quoting fundamentalists not only belong to the church but regard it as an important part of their lives.

This is not to say, of course, that there are not observable similarities among the membership at Immanuel Church. Above all, this is a church of the middle class. The best available statistics indicate that only about 17 percent of SMF's membership are blue-collar workers (as against 26 percent among the Swedish population as a whole), and the percentage of workers at Immanuel Church is probably less (Zetterberg 1979: Table 5.8). SMF is a traditional stronghold of the *folkparti*, the liberal party, the most socially conscious of Sweden's three bourgeois parties. (The other two are the "moderates," Sweden's most conservative party, and the "center," the former agrarian party, which has in recent years stressed ecological causes). In 1978, for example, a year when 12 percent of the Swedish electorate sympathized with the *folkparti*, no less that 45 percent of SMF members named the *folkparti* as their party (Zetterberg 1979: 18, Table 1.1).

Although the core of SMF membership is composed of a strikingly homogeneous middle class, there are also substantial groups on either ideological side of this core. These groups are perhaps especially well represented in Immanuel Church. The location of the church in the middle of Sweden's capital means that its membership is both diverse and variable. There is, to be sure, a stable group of long-time members, but at any time there are also tourists, students, government employees, and business people on temporary assignments participating in the church service. A Sunday morning sermon might have to speak to the recent arrival from the sparsely populated and traditionally communist districts of Sweden's extreme north and at the same time to the 90-year-old Stockholm resident, the sophisticated university student, and the pious youth from the conservative free-church strongholds to the south.

This fact bears directly on the problem discussed in the introduction, namely, the difficulties in considering consensus as a basis for social cohesion. Although the previous pages have pointed to many values and beliefs shared among believers at Immanuel Church, it is also true that on other important religious issues, variation is the norm. It is a *shared* outlook in this church that faith should be personally meaningful; therefore, each believer has a personal perspective on an important symbol of faith like Jesus. It is precisely the point of a personal faith that it should articulate with the most intimate and idiosyncratic details of the believer's life.

This adamant respect for the viewpoint of the individual is itself, of course, an ideological hallmark of the bourgeoisie. This value can be observed in the church's approach to strictly political issues. For example, in April of 1979 an accident occurred in a nuclear reactor at Three Mile Island near Harrisburg, Pennsylvania. For several days, a meltdown of the reactor's core threatened, an eventuality that would have resulted in the release of substantial amounts of dangerous radiation. On the Sunday following the start of this crisis, one of the pastors at Immanuel Church preached a sermon that questioned the safety of nuclear power in strong terms. Nuclear power was an important political issue in Sweden at the time, for a referendum was approaching which would decide the nation's future dependence on nuclear power. Although the pastor stopped short of arguing that a Christian should take a stand against nuclear power, his sentiments were clear to his listeners.

The position he advocated was a liberal one, and based on liberal assumptions.[5] However, probably the most telling middle-class value illustrated here is that of a sort of intellectual laissez-faire. Although the plea was impassioned and the issue a charged one for Swedish citizens, the pastor took care, as mentioned, not to phrase his position in unequivocal terms. He preferred, even on an issue about which he felt strongly, not to tell his parishioners what to think. On most Sundays this stricture is even more carefully observed, and political positions are avoided altogether in favor of vague moral statements open to many interpretations.[6] Thus, the preaching at the Immanuel Church, in adopting a commitment to "objectivity" that transcends almost all other political positions, is classically liberal.

Liberal principles in this sense are also enshrined in church dogma in the form of ecumenism. In theory, at least, no one Christian viewpoint is advocated over any other in SMF. A motion adopted at the 1890 general meeting of SMF specified ecumenism as a fundamental aim of the movement: "SMF has made it its central principle to work for the union of the faithful on the basis of their choice of life in God's son, even though they may have differences of opinion" (Nicklasson 1978: 12). Similarly, today SMF cites as the single criterion for membership "confession of faith in Jesus Christ as Lord and Saviour," emphasizing that none shall be excluded "except for the reason that they lack such faith" (Nicklasson 1978: p. 12).

Even such factors as the design and decoration of the new (dedicated in 1974) building that houses Immanuel Church convey messages about the kind of group that worships here. The new building is an innovative but not imposing structure of modern design. Inside, the sanctuary is noticeable for a high ceiling, skylights, an open, airy feeling, and the effected "roughness" of its inner appointments. The walls, made of unpainted brick, are broken at regular intervals by glass; the effect when the sun is shining is not unlike light seen between the trees in a forest. The pews and lectern are spray-painted green with blotches of yellow and other colors. Here, then, the parishioners sit amidst the colors of the Swedish summer surrounded by soaring walls of rough brick and a feeling of light and openness. In short, the intent is to evoke, with air, light, color, and textures, the great outdoors, the highly prized forests of the nature-loving Swedes.

But this is not really the Swedish outdoors bursting out within this multi-million-dollar building in downtown Stockholm. It is a conscious imitation thereof, and in this situation lies an important insight into SMF. Nature is firmly under control within these walls. It is not *present in* as much as *readmitted* to the building—a wonder of modern design and technology— on the terms of the builders. As pleasant as the woods are, the Swedish wilderness has permitted a decent life to the bulk of its inhabitants for less than a century; nature in this part of the world is beautiful, but for most of the year its beauty is that of harshness, not of benevolence. Nature is dangerous when it is not under control, and it has been the enormous achievement of bourgeois society, in Sweden and elsewhere, to bring nature, in all but its most spectacular vicissitudes, under control.

The sanctuary in Immanuel Church celebrates not only the control over nature but also its return under more orderly circumstances. My familiarity with the old church building, built nearly a century ago (and destroyed in 1977) is limited to photographs, but it was plainly a very different kind of building. A complex facade decorated the exterior of the building; the worship area inside was circular and ornately decorated. Nature was denied in that building, hidden beneath careful and detailed constructions that transformed wood, stone, and glass into an intricate mass of agressively man-made decoration.

It is tempting to draw a larger lesson from this contrast. In sifting through church records in an archive, I once came across an old article about missionary work in Africa complete with "before" and "after" photographs. The first, labeled "witch doctor in heathen ecstasy," showed several individuals framed at odd angles, dressed in native attire and sporting frenzied

The old Immanuel Church, interior

The old Immanuel Church, exterior

The new Immanuel Church, interior

The new Immanuel Church, exterior

expressions. The second, labeled "christian worship," depicts one individual seated in a pew, in Western dress, looking downward with his hand shielding his face. The surrounding pews and walls inscribe straight lines over the whole photograph. The message cannot be missed: to missionize at that time was to bring order, to stamp a pattern on chaotic nature.

In the late nineteenth century, Sweden too was in need of an ordering influence. Alcoholism and tuberculosis were rampant in the slums surrounding industrialized areas, and the workers and rural proletariat, caught in the flux of rapid industrialization, had not much of either tradition or hope. In this context, the message of the new free church and temperance movements, the possibility of renouncing a past life of sin and beginning anew, was a vital and important one. The free churches came to be identified with a strict way of life, the avoidance of the "sins" that were sapping the life of the lower classes: alcohol, distracting entertainments, and a general lack of direction.

In the following generation, this concept of sin remained largely unchanged. But especially among the younger members of Immanuel Church today, the old laundry list understanding of sin seems to have lost its relevance. Most of my friends in the church give little thought to the maxims of thirty years ago, whereby dancing, drinking, playing cards, going to movies, or any sexual activity outside of marriage were thought to be sinful. Instead, they are likely to stress that sin is a matter of how one treats one's fellows. As one woman formulated it—and this statement was heartily endorsed by the ten or so church members of various ages who were listening—sin is that which separates the believer from God or from his fellow persons. Whether or not this position is a change from an earlier outlook, it is rarely these days combined with behavioral strictures at Immanuel Church. Although moral behavior, doing right, continues to be heavily emphasized, doing wrong is not the concern it once was. Today many members react strongly against the old "rules" conception of proper behavior, regarding it as the basis for a stiff and inflexible approach to life that scared people away from the important part of the church's message.

It is hardly strange, then, that the new church building has readmitted nature to its inner sanctum. Order has been established, and it is time to show some quarter to the old antagonist. Social disintegration due to a fragile moral structure is no longer a threat in Sweden, and a more natural and spontaneous style of life is not only acceptable but valued at Immanuel Church. The circumstances of the reappearance of nature, however, make it clear that this is hardly a swing in the direction of hedonism; rather, it is the relaxing of a vigilance that had become anachronistic and constricting.

It is not only in the architecture of the church building and in a general acceptance of spontaneous and not strictly conventional behavior that "nature" is embraced at Immanuel Church. One thing I hope to illustrate in this study is the manner in which commitment entails a relationship between believer and the symbols of faith that is manifestly *physical;* commitment, it will be shown, is literally an *embodiment* of religious symbols.

That Christian faith should have physical manifestations is, of course, no revelation; believers hold that Christ healed the sick and rose from the dead and that the apostles spoke in tongues; medieval mystics entered trances and, in the evangelical tradition of which SMF is a part, a wrenching conversion experience has always been regarded as a sign of grace. At a respectable middle-class institution like Immanuel Church, it is to be expected that the physicality of faith will be manifested in subdued forms, but it is nevertheless an ever-present aspect of the religious life in this congregation.

In succeeding chapters I will discuss this topic as it bears on the question of how believers become committed to their faith. In the remainder of this chapter I will adopt a different perspective and will consider the theme of the physicality of faith as it is expressed in a church service I observed in Immanuel Church.

The service in question, entitled "It is Still Early in the World" (*Ännu är det tidigt i världen*), took place on November 19, 1978. The service did not follow the usual Sunday morning format described above but rather was organized around a number of diffusely defined themes that are recurring concerns of church life. That is, although this service was formally atypical, thematically it was representative of most worship services at Immanuel Church.

In fact, the service seems to have resulted from an attempt on the part of its creators to take familiar messages out of their familiar contexts, so that these messages might once again be heard with the force of the new. As a result, this is particularly apposite service to examine (in spite of its unusual format) in order to demonstrate certain themes that are stressed in the church Sunday after Sunday.

From my experience at Immanuel Church, I would in fact argue that this service was a showpiece, a worship event designed to attract the greatest number of members and outsiders and to demonstrate, to this assembled group, what it is that Immanuel Church has to offer in Swedish society today. Certainly, no expense or effort was spared to make this an innovative and attention-getting worship event. My first surprise came when I walked into the church at the usual time on that Sunday morning, for the building was packed to the rafters, and I had to take a seat on a bench attached to the wall near the back of the church. Many nominal members and interested spectators had evidently arrived at the church to witness the show that was to come; surely, they were not disappointed.

The service was a highly staged and formal event; the music and hymns were all written especially for the occasion, and extensive use was made of dramatic readings and sophisticated electronic sound technology. The music, written and performed by one of Sweden's foremost modern composers, used synthesizers, taped portions, and a string quartet to evoke visions of chaos and power and an overall atmosphere of what I can best describe as "grave eeriness." Although most of the service was presented in the familiar format of a pastor speaking or reading from the front of the church, several sections were recited by an unseen narrator, at times in an unfamiliar language that I later discovered to be Hebrew.

The service starts, appropriately, with the creation. No verbal reference is actually made; rather, a musical piece called "Creation—the Flood" is played. This is an effective means of depicting the beginning of things, for the other-worldly music demands that the listener impose an order in the cacophony, a process that parallels God's work—according to the Bible—in building a world out of chaos. On completion of this five-minute prelude, the following prayer, derived from Psalm 130,[7] is recited in a cadenced speech that I try to recapture here in verse form[8]:

> Out of the deep I call to you Lord
> Lord hear my voice.
> Let your ears
> be attentive to the sound of my prayer.
> If you Lord want to reckon misdeeds
> Lord
> Who can then remain?
> But of course
> we know you grant forgiveness
> for our
> fear of you.

In Swedish, as in English, "the deep" (*djupet*) means, among other things, the deep sea. The title of the piece calls listeners' attention to the waters said by Genesis to exist in the beginning of creation. Thus "the deep" refers here to the waters of chaos, but also the waters from which all of creation emerged. It is likely that those who designed the service, by using the image of "the deep" in the musical context that has been described, were drawing on their knowledge of the primeval cosmology of ancient Israel. Bernhard Anderson, in a book on the Psalms, has described the essentials of this cosmology in a passage worth quoting at some length:

> Israel inherited a picture of the universe which depicted man's world as surrounded on every hand by "the waters of chaos" which, at the time of creation, the Creator subdued and pushed back in order to give man historical space in which to live and to perform his God-given task (Gen. 1: 1 – 2: 41). The earth is portrayed as a kind of island, suspended over the waters of "the deep," within which is located Sheol, the kingdom of death; and beyond the great blue dome overhead are the waters of the heavenly ocean which, unless held back by the protective barrier of the

firmament, would flood the world with chaos (as almost happened, according to the Flood Story)....In the Psalms this language is used religiously or poetically to express man's awareness that on all sides the historical world is threatened by powers of chaos which, were they not held back by the Creator, would engulf man and reduce existence to meaningless confusion. (Anderson 1974: 90)

In subsequent speeches, the "deep" image recurs in various contexts, and its repeated use serves to tie those contexts together. For example, in one section, listeners hear the phrase "from our hearts rises a call of despair.... We are gripped by powerlessness,[9] the waves of darkness and the deep threaten to consume both us and the world." Here "the deep" is associated with threatening *emotions*—despair and powerlessness—and thus located within the self. The deep is also depicted as a pervasive historical theme, as in the following speech, which introduces the reading of the story of Noah[10]:

> Noah and the flood
> is the story of
> how people destroyed
> and misused all the fine things in creation
> and finally how only the flood remained
> that which destroyed almost all life.
> We understand that
> this text also deals with us
> and our own time.

The deep is thus something that occurs in the physical world, in history and within the self. The associations to this point in the service stress further that the deep is chaotic, threatening, frightening. It would be an error to try to specify the meaning of this image too closely, for it is above all *evocative* of a wide range of possible referents. Surely the deep, however, is something disordered, or perhaps disorder itself; it is something mysterious, pervasive, and potentially destructive. As in the Israeli cosmology described by Anderson, the deep is the unfathomable, above which we are suspended.

The unfathomable, that which cannot be known directly, is the void that is everything other than our conscious selves. It is that undifferentiated otherness which is even a component of ourselves in the form of the body and the unconscious. The deep is not death, but death returns us to the deep, for we presume that death is the extinction of our fragile moment of consciousness. This is what I meant when I said that this service seems concerned with matters *physical,* for the deep is an elemental image more visceral than intellectual. One need not devote much thought to the image of the deep in order to feel its ominous power.

However, it is important to recall at this point that Pietism specifies the valid relationship to God as *within,* an ambiguous location that could also be glossed as "underneath." Indeed, it is in the realm of the unfathomable and mysterious that any strong—one may also say "deep"—religious faith must be based. This fact is reflected in a remarkable development in the service in question, an abrupt and total transformation in attitude toward the deep that occurs in the sermon. This passage from the sermon is an expansion on Jesus' words about Noah's contemporaries: "In the days before the flood they ate and drank and married, and they knew nothing until the flood came and swept them all away" (Matthew 24: 39).

> They knew nothing before the flood came.
> The flood.
> The *dark* flood.
> We think of it usually
> as a symbol of destruction,
> it took them all away.
> Our associations go to the creation
> and [indistinguishable]
> the deep abyss[11]
> water of death
> which swallows all.
> And then comes God,
> creator,
> and divides water from water.
> The flood of sin that engulfed Noah
> and his contemporaries
> is a return to the deep from which we departed,
> where life is snuffed out.
> Or we think of the waters of the Red Sea
> which drown the Egyptians along with their evil intentions.
> But the flood of water
> is also a symbol of life.
> The Hebrews went into the Red Sea protected
> by walls of water on their sides
> and toward the promised land.
> Noah was enclosed by God in the ark,
> which was tossed securely
> on the water
> which rose and rose
> and became the most secure ground.

In the transformation from ominous to hopeful associations of the deep image, the modulation from a "minor" to a "major" key (Anderson 1974: 31), an important paradox of faith at Immanuel Church is brought out. A true faith, the service seems to say, is not one that ignores the deep but rather one that does not disdain to embrace life's mystery. A life well-lived is not one that confines itself rigidly to the well-lit paths of the everyday, that attends only to the level of existence that can be controlled and easily understood. Rather, the Christian must not ignore the dark, the terrifying. Death must not be denied. The believer who has enough faith to accept the ultimate void of otherness, says the service, will discover the profound value of the Christian message, that from the horror of destruction comes resurrection.

This principle has appeared before in this book, when Nils Mjönes urged church members to reconceive his disappearance as walking into a painting with Christ. And it will appear again, repeatedly, in the words of individual believers, whose testimony illustrates the drive at Immanuel Church to appropriate faith on a physical level, to build faith in the realm beyond the conscious mind, in the realm of the deep.

In this service, this principle—the mystery of the deep is in a way the foundation of faith—is not *stated,* because to articulate this message would be to undermine it. If it is true that what is most important is beyond words and beyond conscious understanding, the best way to demonstrate this fact is to convey it nonverbally. The service does this by gradually assimilating itself to the form of the very language on which it is based, so that it *reenacts* the stories it tells. The status of the audience thereby shifts from that of listeners to participants; the service is transformed from discourse to experience.

Again, it is likely that this technique has an Israeli inspiration. The image of "the deep" is from a psalm, and most psalms were originally intended for use in worship. Furthermore, as Hermann Gunkel (1928: 269) first pointed out, there is a group of psalms—he referred to them as the Thanksgiving Psalms—characterized by precisely the kind of modulation from desperation to hope that has occurred in this service (see also Anderson 1974: 77ff.). In the thanksgiving pslam, this modulation, in Gunkel's terms "the complete turn about" (*der grosse Umschwung*), reflects God's intervention in the life of the psalmist, rescuing him from a life-threatening situation. The congregation as a whole re-enacts this rescue in the worship service (or ritual) based on the psalm.

The "deep" service is almost certainly modeled after this pattern. The attempt here is to transcend the conventional understanding of scripture as words on a page and not only to perform a series of Scriptural passages but, it is hoped, to involve the audience as participants in the performance. Eerie music, an unfamiliar service structure, and disturbing imagery have been utilized here to stir the emotions of the audience, and the threat of the deep has been linked to their innermost selves. The startling mood shift that occurs in the passage above, then, may be *felt* as a discovery of hope by participants.

The various biblical stories on which the service is built—the creation, the flood, the crucifixion, and resurrection—share a common structure, the movement from chaos and destruction to renewal. In the passage quoted above the service itself begins to conform to the pattern of the stories it tells. Text has become event; image has become reality. The believer who is not only a passive observer but involved in the service finds himself or herself in a position like the Chinese artist depicted in Nils Mjönes's parable, poised between image and reality.

Thus this entire service can be said to constitute a public realization of the basic fact about faith at Immanuel Church: The goal of faith here is commitment, the appropriation of faith not as ideology, not as language, but as experience. The service at once depicts, celebrates, and participates in this basic fact. Moreover, the service uses the mysteries entailed in the experience of commitment to support a perspective on the political responsibilities of the Christian.

This argument, which emerges most strongly after the modulation spoken of above has taken place, has it that the fact that the deep is a source of hope means that the Christian need never despair in the face of evil. The Christian continues to hope, says the service, because he or she knows that the miraculous modulation from death to life may always occur.

In its strongest form, this argument maintains that evil and destruction have no power over the believer, who regards them not as a threat to, but rather as a confirmation of his or her faith:

> When Jesus comes
> it is simply love that comes.
> Not something else.
> Not something grim
> or frightening.
> He comes in order to reveal that most inner and deepest secret
> about the meaning of our life.
> That which is woven into all that we do,
> which is our task
> when we work and live,
> sleep and wake.
> If then the very keynote of existence is love,
> then everything assumes another makeup.
> Then even
> hell has another meaning....
> Hell is nothing other
> than the fire of God's love
> for those that say no
> to it.

Here "the deepest" has become the location of the secret of life, which is love. The most frightening and other has become the most reassuring and the most essential to human life.

This dissolving of the opposition between good and evil would seem at first a technique that might lead to quiesence, an other-worldly focus based on the grounds that this realm is but an illusion. This service, however, adopts the opposite position. The conclusion to be drawn from the fact that conventional oppositions are illusory is that there is hope, that all is not cemented into a grinding, ineluctable progression toward despair. The final message to the believer is that there is hope, and that therefore he or she must act:

> Noah was the only responsible person
> for he cared about the world that God had created.
> He drove into the ark all living species
> so that afterwards the world would have a future.
> He was a man of action.
> And that's something to think about,
> when so many say that one can get to be self-righteous
> if one does things.
> All is of course from grace
> and God's work
> but God has given us responsibility
> and the call to be His co-workers.
> And we cannot ignore that call
> and that responsibility.
> It is important how we think,
> talk
> and act so let us,
> before the flood comes,
> not forget the words of Jesus:
> You will be judged according to your deeds.

Here the vaunted Protestant emphasis on salvation by faith is completely submerged beneath the Pietist stress on the importance of a righteous life. This call to action, fervent yet at the same time absolutely ambiguous as to just what action to undertake, is typical of the preaching at Immanuel Church. Because of its ostensibly apolitical posture, the church rarely if ever recommends particular stands on issues or admonishes the congregation to undertake particular acts. But week after week believers are encouraged to "act."

The logic of this symbolic encouragement is complex. As was pointed out in the previous chapter, SMF has strong strains of social activism in its ideological bloodline but at the same time is heir to a tradition of political

The congregation at worship in the new Immanuel Church

and religious ecumenism. Admirers of this tradition call it freedom of thought; detractors are likely to point out that the refusal to take a stand is always an implicit stamp of approval for the status quo. Suspended between the conviction that Christianity is a this-worldly faith and an equally strong commitment to ideological laissez-faire, preachers at Immanuel Church repeatedly opt for an impassioned plea to act without saying what to do.

It would be an error, however, to rest with this understanding. The call to action is not only a flaccid response to an ideological dilemma. For the invocation of action in general can be seen not only as an admonishment without content, but also as a reference to the concept of human action. Action, after all, is itself something of a mystery, the *realization*—making real—of an intention. It is like the situation depicted in Nils Mjönes's parable: the person conceives something from within and proceeds to make it a part of his or her world. Action in general, then, is an apt symbol for the mystery of grace, a process that involves what I have called commitment, the physical realization of the tenets of faith.

In summary, it could be said that this service as a whole not only *depicts* the situation of the believer at Immanuel Church but also argues for a particular response to that situation. In the service, the believer's dependence on commitment is, as has been shown, reenacted, made a part of the ongoing world. In this context, the admonishment to *act* is nothing other than a command to continue the ritual beyond the walls of the church, to realize the Word not only through the commitment but through the deed as well. And this, as will be shown in the following chapters, is precisely what the believers at Immanuel Church attempt to do in their lives.

4

Symbols Without Meaning

What I have called commitment—or grace, in the words of the believer—is a relationship between the believer and the symbol of faith. By "symbol of faith" here I simply mean to refer to an object, word, or idea that believers use in formulating or practicing their faith, an element of their religious language. The peculiar characteristic of the relationship of commitment is that it is an experience; that is, in grace the symbol is *experienced* by the believer.

I do not expect that this claim, the assertion that one may experience a symbol, will be immediately comprehensible. I recall the first time a believer (an evangelical Christian, but not a member of Immanuel Church) pointed this out to me; my reaction at that time was utter mystification. The woman had told me in no uncertain terms that she *experienced* the words of the Bible. Several times I attempted to get her to reformulate this claim in terms with which I could feel more comfortable. Certain that what she "really meant" was that she experienced situations analogous to those she read about in the Bible, I repeatedly urged her to say this. She was not easily intimidated, however, and continued to assure me that she often experienced the words of the Bible.

Eventually—years, in fact, after conducting that interview—I began to understand what this woman had said. Through the examples contained in the next three chapters, I hope to convey that understanding to the reader. My argument can be to some extent foreshadowed by considering an only partially frivolous analogy. Suppose I were to state that bathing is a relationship between a person and a tub full of water, specifically the relationship of immersion of the person in the water. Presumably, this would be a conceivable assertion. It will also be easy to accept that bathing is an experience.

If I set out to describe bathing, I will be only minimally concerned with specifying the qualities of the bath water. While I may want to mention, say, the temperature of the latter, on the whole my attention will be focused on the person − bath water relationship: how the water feels to the person, what it does to the person, what kinds of activities the person undertakes while immersed in the water, and so on. The significance of religious symbols to which believers are committed is that the believers enter into relationships with those symbols that are like bathing. In a number of ways, believers immerse themselves in the symbols so that the person − symbol relationship is much more than an aspect of thought; it is an experience. In order to describe that experience, one must not limit one's attention to "the symbols themselves"; to do so is like trying to describe bathing by talking exclusively about water.

Thus, I will try to describe commitment as an experience, an ongoing interrelationship between believer and symbol. A good place to begin this task is to examine a believer's words on commitment or, in his terms, grace. I will discuss an article in Immanuel Church's monthly magazine, written by a minister there, entitled "What is grace?" The piece begins with an admission of how difficult it can be to understand a "Christian word" such as grace. The term is difficult to grasp, the author says, because it seems to refer to an abstract world of concepts rather than to the reality we experience in our everyday lives. As one might expect, this statement is used to introduce a discussion of how grace *is* in fact a reality present in experience:

> Grace is a summons, a challenge to live in truth and love. To receive God's grace is therefore to commit oneself to[1] a rich life under God's direction and power, for God's grace is actually Christ and his presence entails a possibility to find oneself and one's purpose.

There are a number of points I would like to make with reference to this short passage. In the first place, note that the author identifies grace with commitment: "to receive God's grace is therefore to commit oneself." This illustrates an equivalence I have been depending on since the first chapter: grace with commitment: "to receive God's grace is therefore to commit oneself." This illustrates an equivalence I have been depending on since the first chapter: grace equals commitment. Commitment is a word that is used in the church in the same way I am using it in this book, as a non-spiritual synonym for grace. The difference between the two terms is one of perspective. The believer, the person who experiences commitment, construes that experience above all else as being of God. It should always be kept in mind that what I describe, from the outside, as commitment, the believer interprets as the presence of God. No matter what other regularities are observed in the operation of commitment in this church, this one will remain paramount: through experiences of commitment widely diverse orientations are synthesized into a common discourse. All commitment is, to believers, evidence of the efficacy of God. But this common discourse is forged out of diverse meanings rather than shared ones; it is precisely the perceived intervention of the divinity in the idiosyncratic details of a biography that empowers the image of God in this church.

The second feature of this passage I want to note is the enigmatic "God's grace is actually Christ." This statement is intended to be evocative rather than transparent; grace, like Christ, is a free gift of God, and both are manifestations of God on this plane. It is through grace, and through Christ, that the believer is saved. Furthermore—and this point is essential in the present context—grace is like Christ in entailing a literal *embodiment* of divinity. The terms of that embodiment are specified in the passage: grace is to commit oneself, and to find one's self and one's purpose.

Grace, then, is to *embody* one's true self and purpose, and thereby to be transformed. It is to realize, to make real, that which had previously been only an ideal (or an idea). It is typical that grace is referred to here as a *possibility,* that is, as a juncture in experience where one may choose commitment and one's true self. This dual possibility is familiar from another context, the literature on the Christian "conversion experience." The consistent, if paradoxical, claim of the convert is, "I gave myself up and thereby found myself." St. Augustine, for example, was converted to Christianity in the moment he submitted to what he regarded as a command of God—which appeared in a Bible verse—to abandon the very vices to which he had previously clung most tenaciously (Augustine 1961: p. 178). In giving up his willful self, Augustine informs us, he found light, knowledge, and happiness such as he had never before experienced.

In talking to members of Immanuel Church, I was initially surprised by how *little* I heard about the significance of such "conversions" among the members, for I knew that in the early years of the church these experiences had been the very center of church life. Gradually, however, I came to suspect that the conversion experience had not so much disappeared as been *transformed* into an experience that was less clearly defined, the experience of grace.

What I mean by "less clearly defined" can best be illustrated by an example. I once heard a vigorous believer in her late fifties comment that becoming aware of the women's movement and making that awareness a part of her life were so expanding of her "possibilities" that they produced a feeling much like a conversion experience.

Although hearing the liberating message of the women's movement is not a spiritual experience in any sense, this woman linked it to the explicitly spiritual conversion because both are "expansions of possibilities." Many church members would not go so far as this woman, who is somewhat outspoken. Normally, when church members referred to an experience of grace using the word "possibility," their descriptions contained some reference to God or the Bible. But this example points to the fact that there is something other than the ineffable feeling of God's presence which marks not only the conversion but the personal commitment to *any* symbols which seem to the person to express something vital about the self, as the symbols of the women's movement did for this believer. To see the profound significance of a symbol or set of symbols for one's life is to see something new about oneself, a *possibility* of which one had not previously been aware. Whether or not the symbols in such an experience are spiritual ones, and whether or not the experience has the overwhelming power of a personal conversion, the fundamental mechanism of commitment entails a change in perspective on one's self that links any experience of grace (in the way I am using the term) to the form of the transforming conversion.

I have in fact suggested elsewhere (Stromberg 1985) that the experience of "finding oneself" in a symbol system is a widespread symbolic process which can be labeled (using a term from the work of Wilhelm Dilthey) as the experience of an "impression point." The essence of this argument is that it is possible for a person to experience a moment of almost physical merger with a symbol, a moment in which the person "finds himself" in a symbol that had, an instant before, been merely an object of thought. In other words, a relationship of commitment occurs when the symbol and the self are, at least momentarily, merged. Such a relationship therefore always entails the *possibility* of self-transformation, because it enables the self to be seen in terms of the symbol it has collapsed into.

This latter point is, at least in part, what the minister who wrote on grace wished to say to his congregation. Grace is a possibility for commitment and transformation, for establishing a relation to the symbol that entails a highly personal meaningfulness for the believer.[2] Note here that I do not say *meaning*, for such a relationship is not necessarily articulable, and it is certainly not significant mainly as a vehicle for communication to others.

The essential point here is rather that a believer may enter into a relationship of identification with a symbol. Such a relationship entails a bond of sentiment between person and the symbol which has come to partake of the significance of the self. It is the existence of this bond of sentiment, I would hold, that constitutes what has been called an "inner" relationship between believer and symbol.

The possibility of such a relationship being established is dependent in turn upon the conception of "inner" or "deep" meanings of the religious symbols. It is only on the basis of such inner meanings that the symbol can appear as so perfectly adapted to the idiosyncracies of personal experience that a relation of identification can be established.

Thus, again, "God's grace is actually Christ." Grace, like Christ, is a manifestation of the divine power that reconciles the believer with the religious symbol (through the process of identification). It is that mystery in which the corporeal and the transcendent meet. This conjunction has been encountered before in these pages, in the first place in the parable told by Nils Mjönes. In the present context, the point is that grace, or commitment, is a process in which the symbolic becomes real, in which it attains the status of experience. Thus grace becomes also a possibility, a possibility to encounter the transcendent, and in that encounter, to be transformed.

Having thus sketched out at least part of the fundamental logic of grace, I would now like to illustrate how all this works in the lives of believers. It is my intention, above all, to demonstrate how grace is manifested in the lives of believers, or, from another perspective, to show how the very selves of believers are shaped by processes of commitment.

The next several chapters will present material from conversations I had, or my research assistant had,[3] with members of Immanuel Church. I have organized the chapters around certain patterns I noticed in the ways believers used religious language and in the way they see God as manifesting himself in their lives. Each chapter demonstrates how such a pattern can be reduced to a relationship between religious language and self; in a sense, then, the following chapters describe three ways in which religious language shapes selves in Immanuel Church.

The first set of ideas I will discuss is that expressed by a man I will call Per. (Per, like all the people I discuss in this book, is an actual individual, a member of Immanuel Church, although I have changed his name and certain identifying information.) Per, who is in his late thirties, earns his living as an engineer; he is married and the father of four. He grew up in a strict religious home. Per is an active participant and leader in devotional activities in the church; he and his wife give much of their time and energy to groups that study the Bible and reflect on personal problems from a Christian standpoint.

Per's conception of how God influences his action, indeed his whole idea of what it is to be a good Christian, is summed up in his oft-repeated remark that the Christian must "obey God's plan." On one level, this expression simply means that the believer must follow the commands recorded in the Bible. For example, Per believes God has concrete ideas about the institution of marriage:

> God created us in body and soul and spirit, and decreed, among other things, that we should work. Now we can also say he instituted mar-
> riage. And marriage, in his opinion, is one man and one woman who

stand up for their whole life to support each other and meet each other's needs.

However, obedience to God entails much more than just obeying his commands. God has a plan for each *individual,* and living according to God's will means that one must discern and follow that plan:

> It's important that we realize that even though we can go our own way, God has another plan for us. And since he loves us he has the possibility to reconcile [his plan and our own].... But this means we've got to see, got to confess our sins and be willing to subordinate ourselves... under God's will, and receive him as our Saviour.

How does one discern God's plan so that one may follow it? Per believes he must memorize Bible verses, thereby storing God's Word within himself. He has faith that in moments of indecision he can consult God's Word as it is recorded in his memory and that he will light upon a verse that will show him the way to proceed. After his conversion, Per says, God's Word:

> began to form a basis... and then I began to learn these verses by heart—"I have given you this in order that you shall know," right?—and I stick to (*hålla fast till*) that when the time comes, and then I'm holding myself (*hålla mig till*) to Jesus' Word, and I can keep myself uncorrupted, so to speak, and not go wrong.

In order to show in detail how Per uses the Bible and prayer in order to discern God's plan and to illustrate the benefits he finds in doing so, I will now consider a series of events from his life that he reported in some detail during the interview.

This story concerns a set of circumstances at Per's place of employment. It is easy to discern, listening to Per, that he is a conscientious worker. In fact, as he says, he is the type who would err on the side of overdoing his job, of not being sufficiently relaxed and flexible. Before the conversion experience that reoriented his faith and his life, Per says, he used to pray to God to help him make great discoveries. He wanted his work to bring benefits to mankind, but he had set ideas about how this was to come about.

After the conversion, however, Per began to think of his work, and God's participation therein, in another way. He says:

> I believe... that he [God] wants to help us do a job well. Not so that it's really easy, that you get it done really easily, or that you get really high praise for the job or whatever, that you're a fantastic engineer. But in that it becomes a good job where you're happy because what you do is useful, and that work won't pressure you so much that you can't manage anything else. I don't believe that's God's will.

Such an outlook is eminently reasonable and, one imagines, a noticeable improvement over a time when Per felt tremendous pressure to produce. But although such a view of things is a good general theory, there are stressful times when such generalities are insufficient comfort. Per goes on to talk about such a time:

> When I began at my job there were many things... that weren't good at all. I almost got ulcers... and every Monday morning I felt sick to my stomach and sometimes I couldn't sleep at night.

Per's response to this situation was, together with his wife, to attempt to bring his problems to the attention of God. They decided to make a detailed list of exactly what was bothering him, right down to the aspects of particular projects that were difficult. Then, while he was at work, his wife prayed about the details on the list, one by one. "And the Lord began to solve one thing after another," says Per. In this way, the immediate crisis was surmounted.

Per was convinced that this method would succeed because he feels it is so promised in the Bible; that is, he was certain that the procedure he followed was in concert with God's plan. Such crises, however, continued to arise. Some time later Per was given a more responsible position at his firm, a position that entailed more administrative work than he felt comfortable with. His new duties were a strain, and several times he almost blew up on the job. He also contemplated quitting:

> First I thought like, "should I change jobs or what?" But then this verse came to me, that we should subordinate ourselves to our superiors and serve them with all out hearts as if they were Christ.... There was a sort of middle-level manager who was causing most of the trouble... [so] I decided to be subordinate to him, to have faith in my superiors there. So six months later, without my doing anything, he got another job, and a new manager, who had a much better administrative sense, replaced him. And this guy changed my situation so that it was much better.

This description captures an essential feature of what Per is talking about when he discusses "following God's plan," for that process always entails yielding to outside authority. Per's interview constantly returns to the themes of authority and control, one example of such concerns being his authoritarian ideas of marriage. He is clearly a person quite concerned with these issues, and thus it is interesting that for him, following God's plan— and thus receiving grace—occurs when he yields his own authority to someone else.

As with the conversion, this yielding of authority—whether to God or to a superior on the job—leads to a situation that is better, less conflict-ridden, more true to the way things should be. In the terms I have been using, Per finds a more satisfactory self, a better integration into the world, by yielding his self-control to something outside himself, ultimately to God. In so doing, he feels, he is able to transcend his own limited view and grasp a truer understanding of himself and his situation. An outside observer might confirm Per's assessment of the benefits of yielding some control over the situations he encounters, while perhaps offering a different explanation of these benefits. Simply put, Per is a person who has a tendency to try to control things, to exercise authority, and his faith obviously helps him to recognize this tendency and to some extent to avoid it.

What might—somewhat misleadingly—be termed Per's "style of interpretation" is in fact a direct outgrowth of the way he experiences grace. In discussing grace as a possibility, I noted that the foundational feature of the experience of grace is the discovery of "possibilities" for the self, the renewal of hope through a changed perspective on who one is. For Per, finding himself in the symbols of his faith—the verses of the Bible—occurs in a particularly stark and unembellished fashion. He sees those verses as literal and unambiguous commands to which he must conform.

As a result, these verses are often not attributed "meanings" which are regarded as appropriate for the religious community as a whole. Although— as his comments on marriage demonstrate—Per is convinced that the Bible contains instructions for humanity in general, the bulk of his interest is devoted to those instances in which Bible verses speak directly to him, to situations that are unique rather than universal.

In a sense, any discussion of "meanings" is simply inappropriate to the issue of how Per relates to the Word of God. That verses have "meanings" suggests a level of articulable conceptions which stand between the formulations of the Bible and Per's experience. But for Per, the whole point is to seek to avoid such mediation, to *live* the words of the Bible, to make them a part of his experience:

> You can't really study [the Bible]; instead you've got to begin in some way: take one thing you understand, apply that in faith to God, and have faith that God will bless it.... When you're faced with a choice and you say, "Okay, now I'm going to stick to (*hålla fast till*) this and... trust in you, [Lord]."

Per relates to the words of the Bible in a manner that is distorted by the rhetoric of meaning and interpretation. His hope and constant goal are that the Word shall *constitute* his experience. Per's literal, or as he would put it, "concrete" understandings of Bible verses are an attempt to avoid the mediating level of interpretation as that which reconciles the Word with his life.

As seems always to be the case in a faith that is well thought out (Stromberg 1981b), Per's stance on the Word is reflected in his ideas about Jesus. Per holds that Jesus, like the Word, must be appropriated by the believer in an almost physical union, so that his features constitute experience. This claim is best demonstrated in Per's description of his conversion experience. Per, having been brought up in a religious home, had always had a strong faith in God. But his faith remained, he says, something distant and partial, a belief that there was an afterlife, a hope for God's assistance in times of need.

Then, at a time of crisis in his life, when he had just broken up with a woman he had hoped to marry and was beginning to find his relations with his fellow students unsatisfactory, he ran into a Christian friend who urged him to pray to Jesus to come into his heart. Per took the advice, and he found that it changed his whole view of Christianity. Here is Per's description of his conversion:

> There was an occurrence when I was about 25, where I got to surrender myself to Christ in a special way. I think I had a Christian faith, a faith in Christ as my Saviour, earlier. But then... I decided that "starting now, it will be what Jesus thought and believed in that will be what I set the most weight on," so to speak. Not what I read in the newspapers or saw on TV or what I myself figured out, but what Jesus thought was worthwhile, I decided to follow that. And then it became a whole different stage in my life, from what it was earlier... [when I had] wanted to have something to do with Jesus but, well, I tried to determine myself how much he would get to do with me, if I could express it that way.... You could say that before I had understood that Jesus had died for my sins. I didn't need to be afraid of death. But no possibility that people's *lives* could be so different from every normal John Doe's here on earth.... Suddenly there was a possibility to get out the power of Jesus' resurrection, victory over temptation and a meaning in what you do here, in this world. It was as if the resurrection part of his life, so to speak, moved up to a possibility that could be realized here and now.

The two features of this passage that are especially relevant here are, first, the fact that the conversion occurs when Per decides to submit totally to Jesus, to become obedient to what Jesus "thought and believed in." Conversion follows from an obedience that amounts to a replacing of Per's own will by that of Jesus. Second, note the consequence of the conversion: the "*possibility* to get out the power of Jesus' resurrection, victory over temptation and meaning in what you do here, in this world" (my emphasis). The effect of Per's rebirth is to appropriate the power of Jesus' rebirth, his resurrection; the point is that in essence Per conceives his conversion as an echo of, perhaps even a *re-living* of, the experience of Christ.

Through his conversion, Per established a relation of identification with Jesus that yielded not a particular meaning but a *source* of meaning, a *power* to overcome temptation and to *find* meaning in life. It is this complex of identification, emotion, and power that constitutes what the Pietists referred to as an inner relationship to Christ, and that I have designated commitment. For Per, the experience of grace typically assumes the form of stepping beyond his own volition; it is this *possibility,* and the further possibilities thereby entailed, that form the center of his faith.

I would now like to discuss another believer who, although very different from Per, seems to share some of his fundamental ideas on volition and grace. She too assigns profound significance to the experience of transcending her own volition; her commitment to Christ can be clearly linked to such experiences. In addition, her faith provides a striking demonstration of the refusal to embrace meaning as a mediator to God, in that this woman (alone among the people we interviewed at Immanuel Church) reported that she speaks in tongues. The implications of this activity for the question of meaning as a mediator to God will be discussed below.

Elisabet is a 21-year-old nursery school teacher and is unmarried. She grew up in SMF and joined the church at age 14. Like many people who were raised in the church, she cites a two-week long summer confirmation camp as important in her decision to officially join SMF. (Perhaps the most important feature of such camps, attended by young adolescents, is a not-too subtle social pressure to conform by becoming a Christian through some sort of visible "commitment to Jesus.")

In Elisabet's case, the influence of the camp was compounded by another factor. Shortly before she was to leave for the camp, she had a conversation with her grandfather in which he emphasized the need to join the church (*församling*) because of the togetherness and social contact it offers. In his words, the church provides security, is like "a second home." It turned out that this was the last time Elisabet spoke with her grandfather, for he died shortly thereafter. This turn of events affected Elisabet strongly: "This [her grandfather's death] was a shock, and it made me think about our talk. That's what led to my decision to join [SMF]."

Like Per, Elisabet stresses the importance for her faith of direct contact with God. She says she feels her religion as:

> a daily communion (*gemenskap*) with God.... It means so much that sometimes I wonder, what *is* this I believe in? Just think, what if God doesn't exist? After all, I can't see him. And all the other things that non-Christians bring up. But then I realize how dumb it is to think that way, because God has helped me so many times, I experience his presence in such a real way.

In other respects, Elisabet's faith differs noticiably from Per's. Although she too reads the Bible and regards it as the Word of God, she does not emphasize the kind of specific correspondences between verses and experience with which Per is so concerned. She too has seen such correspondences, but they are not the center of her faith.

Rather, Elisabet stresses that the feeling of direct contact with God, through prayer and speaking in tongues, is ultimately more salient for her than Bible reading. For instance, she says that if she is having trouble with something in her life, she is unlikely to go to the Bible for help, for one thing because it may be difficult to find a section that deals with the problem she is having at that moment. So, says Elisabet, "If there's a problem, I'm more likely to go to God directly, instead of the Bible." She formulates the difference between prayer and Bible reading as follows:

[The Bible] is God's Word. It's where we get our faith from. I have to read the Bible if I'm going to learn anything.... The Bible is there so we can read God's Word, [while] we have prayer to come closer to God, nearer in togetherness with him. I think that you can learn to know God through the Bible. But you can't get near him like you can through prayer. Because that's a conversation with God.

God comes to Elisabet much less often as words than as feelings. I pointed out that Per's relation to God's Word represents a striving to live the words directly, to dispense with an intermediate level of meaning, of interpretation. Elisabet shows a tendency to take this form of relation one step further and to dispense with words altogether. She says of her faith:

It's a security I experience. And then also, that he helps me, in my day-to-day life. If I have a hard time at my job, I can pray to God in these situations where I can't make it by myself (*jag klarar det inte själv*). And then I pray to God and I notice that it's solved, and I don't know *how*. But it's so *obvious*, I feel it as so near.

The abandonment of meaning is demonstrated above all in Elisabet's tongue-speaking. Speaking in tongues is vocalization which the believer experiences as spontaneous and not under his or her conscious control. In some Christian contexts, speaking in tongues is interpreted as a manifestation of the Holy Spirit in accord with the Biblical description of Pentecost (Acts 2: 4). The actual utterances of the tongue-speaker are presumed to be some language, unfamiliar to the speaker, which may or may not (depending on the beliefs of the group and the particular situation) be interpretable by the speaker or by specially gifted listeners.

The literature on tongue-speaking stresses that the phenomenon is most likely to occur in group settings, at times and in places associated with the activity. Such was not the case for Elisabet; she stresses that the situation she was in when she "received the gift of tongues"

wasn't remarkable at all. I was with a friend at the house of a member of the congregation who is fifty or sixty years old. She is very firm in her faith. We were out in the country, she and I, sitting and talking and swimming, and then I got the speaking in tongues. No big overflowing happening or anything, it was just calm and natural.

Elisabet has spoken in tongues many times since that day in the country, and she finds that doing so brings her substantial comfort of the type she mentioned earlier, security and support:

It [speaking in tongues] fills me with strength in some way. Sometimes you can feel somehow like Satan isn't trying to tempt you or make you unhappy in certain situations.

Again, Elisabet's faith functions here in a way that is both like and unlike Per's. Per had his conversion once; the logic of the event dictates that it should not recur repeatedly. However, as was shown, the continuous experience of "following God's plan" is in its main features a repetition of the conversion, in that it is a reception of grace following from the subordination of Per's will to that of the Lord.

There is no reason why the experience of tongue-speaking cannot occur again and again. In this the structure of Elisabet's faith differs from Per's. However, she, like Per, points to a fundamental similarity between the special experience of grace in a moment of ecstasy, and its more commonly experienced manifestations. Both provide her with security through a feeling of God's nearness.

Furthermore, like Per, Elisabet attributes her ability to receive God's grace to her yielding her volition to God. No human activity is more tightly tied to the will than is language; although one can *desire* without being able to put the desire into words, to *will* seems to necessitate a putting into words. In this sense, volition and articulate expression are inexorably linked. To articulate is the fundamental act through which will is formulated. To have the experience of speaking, then, but at the same time to have the sense that the words are not one's own, is surely a profound experience of subordination to another will. This is precisely how Elisabet describes speaking in tongues:

It [speaking in tongues] feels like now it's just me and God. Now it's we who talk—or [that's not right, it's not] we who talk—*he* puts the words in my mouth, I actually don't know what I'm saying, but still I feel that this is something direct.

Elisabet's momentary confusion here results directly from the paradoxical logic of speaking in tongues. She starts by classifying speaking in tongues as speaking to God, then retracts this formulation as she realizes its insufficiency. Rather, she says, "*he* puts the words in my mouth." The point is that Elisabet experiences speaking in tongues both as speaking, exercising her own will, and being controlled by the will of God. In speaking in tongues, her will and the will of God are one.

That meaning is conspicuously absent from this relation is demonstrated by the form of tongue-speaking, the vocalization of "words" that have no meaning. The utterance of the tongue-speaker, like the Bible verse for Per, is significant first of all not because of its potential interpretation, but rather because it is a form wherein the believer may dwell with God. In such forms, some aspect of the conscious self and something outside the conscious self—something of God, according to the believer—are momentarily merged.

For both Per and Elisabet, the mysterious processes whereby words that they have not themselves formulated come to them are the strongest possible evidence of grace, of the presence of God in their lives. Although the observer may not regard these processes as evidence of the action of any divinity, the processes themselves are nevertheless present (people in fact *do* speak in tongues and have conversions) and undeniably somewhat mysterious. The minimal conclusion must be that religious symbols intervene in the lives of the faithful not only through conscious processes such as interpretation but through unconscious processes that this account only begins to describe. As a result of these processes, religious symbols can enter into believers' lives at the level of the given, the unquestionable, the level of experience.

Although the transformation from symbol to lived reality is evidently a defining feature of the experience of grace at Immanuel Church, the details of that transformation vary widely among the church membership. In fact, the form I have just described is not widespread in Immanuel Church; I turned to it first because it is such a clear example of the fundamental logic of grace in the church. In the next chapter I will describe a type of faith that is much more typical of the church membership, an understanding of grace that provides some room for a conception of meaning.

5

Discovering the Self

In beginning the previous chapter, I noted that the experience of grace—that is, the forging of commitment to the symbols of faith—occurs in Immanuel Church in a number of forms, forms by no means limited to the traditional evangelical "conversion" experience. In this chapter I would like to expand this observation by examining the faiths of three believers who demonstrate a second general approach to the experience of grace. These believers all experience grace in discovering, in some way, the potentialities of the self. Although such an outlook may initially sound excessively individualistic, in practice this perspective is usually accompanied by a conviction that such potentialities are discovered only in interaction with other people. Thus, these believers share with those discussed in the previous chapter the fundamental idea that grace is a *realization* of the self at the same time as it is a *transcendence* of the self.

Ideas about grace and the discovery of the self—and this is in contrast to the ideas described in the previous chapter—are pervasive in the church. Thus, the ideas expressed by the believers quoted in this chapter represent positions that most church members would endorse. As I pointed out earlier, however, there is a difference between claiming that an outlook is widespread or typical in a group and claiming that that outlook is an element of consensual culture as the latter term is normally understood. One way to formulate this distinction is to rely upon a concept suggested by the French social theorist Pierre Bourdieu (1977: 15), that of a "cultivated disposition."

Bourdieu (p. 14) points out that we may observe that a group of people continually resort to characteristic ideas about preserving honor, for example, but that it is a distortion to conceive this fact as though the "abstract principle" of equality in honor were itself ordering the behavior of group members. To do so would be to displace agency from actors and locate it in principles; in such a conceptualization the persons concerned with honor are but puppets manipulated by an abstract principle. Instead, suggests Bourdieu, honor should be seen as the emergent creation of a community of persons who share a sense of honor embedded in habitual dispositions and postures. The characteristic ideas that the observer notes and summarizes under the rubric of "the honor system" are the result of regularities in the way the members of the community learned to be human: to walk, to converse, to express emotion. The members of the community (in my own terms now) are veritably *constituted* by their attachment to certain social forms, some of which lead to patterns of behavior that may be called the system of honor. But that system is a generalization derived from the observation of behavior, not a cause of behavior.

In the same way, there is an important distinction between describing patterns of grace and attributing to those patterns the mysterious autonomy and efficacy that have been claimed by those who assume that "culture is consensus." In the following discussion, I will show that believers at Immanuel Church commonly elaborate on the fundamental position that God helps them to recognize and realize their potentialities as people, but this should not be taken to mean that this fundamental position causes any person's action.

In offering the alternative conceptualization of "cultivated dispositions," I mean to call attention to the fact that such a believer's characteristic ideas may be most usefully thought of as so deeply embedded in his or her approach to the world that they are as much what we call physical as what we call mental. Again a phrase from Bourdieu is apposite, for he discusses such dispositions as "embedded in the agents' very bodies" (1977: 15). From this perspective, the assertion that believers develop characteristic under*stand*ings of religious symbols has an important double meaning.

In my own observations, these embedded understandings may be manifested as extraordinarily consistent patterns of conception in the believer's thought, patterns of which the believer is not aware. Such patterns are exemplified by both the believers discussed in the previous chapter. It was pointed out there that Per consistently seeks a "closeness" to the symbols of his faith. In the area of Bible reading, this manifests itself in literal interpretations. In his relationship to Jesus, this closeness appears in the guise of a conversion experience that amounts to an almost physical union, a re-living of certain aspects of Jesus' experience. This parallel is not a result of Per's conscious intention; rather, it is a manifestation of a deeply entrenched pattern of thought. This pattern is in the way Per organizes ideas, in his mechanism of thinking. In this sense such a pattern could be called a *posture*, a stance in experience. It may even be useful to think of such a pattern not as a phenomenon of the mind but of something that operates on a more basic level than the mind because it *organizes* the mind.

It is helpful to conceive of the profound experience of the conversion, the emotional center of Per's faith, as a physical experience of a mental pattern. In the conversion Per's approach to religious symbolism is appropriated on the level of the *body,* with all the consequences of permanence and undoubted reality that the body (in contrast to the mind) entails. Per himself, in describing his conversion, calls attention to the fact that that event entailed a shift away from a symbolism that was part of his intentional thought and toward one that was beyond the level of intention. Before the conversion, he says, he "wanted to have something to do with Jesus but, well, I tried to determine myself how much he would get to do with me, if I could express it that way."

Elisabet's faith, of course, provides another example of the point. For her, speaking in tongues—an activity that clearly stands on the boundary between the body and mind—expresses in a physical experience the pattern of integrating God's power into her life. Thus, to observe the faith of these two believers is to see, in the clearest manner, that faith may exist not only in thought but beyond thought. Faith exists both in actual physical manifestations and in unconscious, non-intentional processes that organize what we call the mind.

I will now discuss a third example, a believer who has not been previously introduced. He is a 27-year-old accountant named Anders who has been very active in church life, serving in important positions in the church youth group, SMU.[1] Like many members of Immanuel Church, Anders is something of a political activist, although he stresses that he tries to direct himself to local and immediate problems: "The political consequences of Christianity should above all manifest themselves in the immediate environment, I think. Maybe it seems like I'm making the whole thing too individual or private, but that's what I think."

Thus, Anders directs his energies into intrachurch politics or just greeting new people that come to church:

> I want to be so open that when they [non-church members] want me to, I'll be ready to stand up. When you meet new folks in the church it's important to show an interest in them, to stand up and talk and tell them about what the congregation is doing and so on. I've done this many times with people who are new in the church. I've shown them around the church, chatted with them, told about what we do. This is something I think is important for getting the congregation to function.

The theme of attending to the specific situation rather than the grand levels of generality also typifies Anders's approach to Bible reading. Like Per, he holds that it is in the situations of actual living that the meanings of Bible verses will emerge:

> If you read [the Bible] regularly it sort of builds up some kind of capital so that then, if you encounter a situation, then you've got a basis in the Word of the Bible and Christian values at the bottom that you've built up, so that you feel like "this is God's meaning" and "this is God's will."

It is possible to be more specific about this pattern of thought that is beginning to be noticeable in Anders's words. Again and again, speaking of a variety of issues, Anders formulates his positions in a way that stresses an underlying pattern: Insight, meaning, truth, and God himself are embedded *within* the forms one encounters in the world, and, if one has faith, these qualities will *emerge* from those forms. For example, when asked when he feels the need to pray, Anders responded that it is often "stuff that happens in the world and society" which provokes him to prayer in an attempt to understand the (inner) meaning of events which seem, on the face of it, meaningless. Consider his comments on a television show he saw, an American-made drama of the fate of a Jewish family in Hitler's Germany:

> When I see something like this "holocaust" program, there I feel like I need to pray and ask questions, because I don't understand how such an evil can come to power. I've got to struggle with my faith before God (*brottas inför Gud*).

Confronted with a situation so unqualifiably evil as the holocaust, Anders treats it as a puzzle. He approaches the great paradoxes of faith in a similar way; he commented on the crucifixion of Jesus, "It's hard for us to conceive the *innermost* aspects of this" (my emphasis).

At the same time, Anders believes that God consistently works in different areas of life to help the "innermost" emerge. The situations or events one actually encounters in life may then be seen as edifices within which God's Word resides and is mediated to believers. Anders thinks of the sermon in this way, for example:

> I listen to a sermon as God's Word *refracted through a human*. Do you understand what I mean? Exactly like you can *refract light through a prism*. It's something that's *transported via a person,* but the person's character will play a big role in the message which is *brought forth*. I don't believe that people don't play a role, that God speaks directly, so to speak. That's not the way I experience a sermon; rather it's God *reflected through a person*. And that God can use a person's character and characteristics to *bring out* certain things which are [his Word]. (my emphasis)

Anders articulates particularly well in this passage the process whereby God's meaning is "brought forth" into the world. He compares the individual to the cut of a prism's sides, which enables it to refract light. A particular person, like a particular configuration of events, can serve as the vehicle whereby God's meaning emerges into the world.

The most important event whereby God's meaning emerged into the world, in Anders's view, is of course in the life, death, and resurrection of Jesus. It is not surprising, then, that these same themes can be observed in Anders's description of Jesus' death. He conceives that event using various images of forming an *opening* through which meaning was made available to humankind:

> Jesus' death on the cross is, you could say, *an opening in the wall,* if I can express myself so.[2] Those symbols or occurrences which happened on Good Friday and Easter can be taken as symbols for things that happened as a result. *The curtain tearing in the temple...* the distance between God and humankind disappeared...God is our personal God in another way. And at the same time, *the mountain burst,* or whatever it says in the Bible. Then *the kingdom of the dead opened,* and we got a chance to *escape out of the jaws of death.* (my emphasis)

Thus, the attention to "the inner" that characterizes various aspects of Anders's faith consists of two fundamental tenets. First, there is the attention to the specific situation or event as receptacle in which God's Word is somehow embedded. Then there is the conviction that, through some unnamed and presumably unfathomable process, God's Word will *emerge* and present itself to the believer.

In his belief that the symbol in Christianity has an inner meaning, Anders is of course testifying to his Pietist heritage. And it is not only the symbols of faith that conform to this pattern, but aspects of the environment as well. The pattern of thought that has been described here is in fact so pervasive in Anders's thought that it imparts a consistent cast to his mental process.

In this sense, the pattern of "meaning emerging from inside" is what was referred to earlier as a disposition.[3] It is a stance in the world of thought; over time this stance defines a *style* of thought. This disposition, this style, is a manifestation of grace, for it is a relationship between Anders and the broad range of events and situations he regards as signs of his faith. The form of this relationship is one of commitment, in that it is a pre-articulate constituent of Anders's identity. But this disposition is usefully understood as a manifestation of grace from Anders's perspective as well, for it is the manner in which God consistently appears in his life.

In other words, the style that has been located in Anders's thought is self-reinforcing. When Anders observes some phenomenon which might plausibly be interpreted along the lines that have been outlined, he is likely to seize the opportunity. Doing so, he is likely to be struck by a deep and profound sense of significance, for his observations will resonate with pervasive patterns in his thought.

It was shown above how this happened to Per in his conversion, and to Elisabet, when she speaks in tongues. Anders's faith does not manifest itself in a similarly spectacular configuration. However, his faith is not for that reason any less deep or emotionally full than that of the believers discussed previously. Consider, for example, Anders's response to a religious rock opera he watched recently. He was moved by a final scene in the opera, a scene which he felt expressed Christ's most important message to humanity. The play depicted Christ, in taking leave of his apostles, as citing something unique characterizing each one of them. For Anders, this expressed the truth that Christ came to earth in part to help each individual discover and express his or her inner essence. As he states in characteristic imagery in another part of his interview: "I think God has an intention for all persons, all persons have a character that God wants to *bloom forth*" (my emphasis).

In viewing this drama, then, Anders had a moment of profound insight of the type that has been labeled an experience of grace. Not only is the insight itself valuable, but it reflects in its form deeply embedded patterns in Anders's thought. One can understand how such an experience, which is both an example of and a symbol for a fundamental disposition that is constitutive of Anders's very uniqueness and identity as a person, may very well strike him as a manifestation of divinity.

This example also demonstrates the characteristic that Anders shares with other believers described in this chapter, and indeed with many church members: a tendency to find the confirming experience of grace in the process of "discovering the self." I noted above that few of the believers I talked to—in presumed contrast to what would have been the case a century ago—mentioned a "conversion" experience as the emotional or intellectual center of their faith. On the other hand, most believers referred to *some* kind of experience that "summed up" their faith, some experience that seemed to them a particularly telling example of the process of grace, of God's efficacy in their lives.

Per and Elisabet found such experiences in transformations of an almost physical nature that entailed the feeling of yielding their volition. Anders, on the other hand, cites no such example, but stresses a milder form of self-transformation, the discovery of innate *possibilities* within the self. He cites this as the center of what the Christian message has to offer in today's world:

> It would...give everyone a bigger chance for personal harmony and satisfaction, that I'm worth something, I'm worth something for what I am. People wouldn't need all those justifications like "I'm good at conversation," "I'm intelligent," or "I've had a successful career," or whatever. Rather they could seize on what they are, that's enough.

Anders's conception of the self thus parallels his outlooks on the situations of everyday life, the sermon, the great puzzles of existence, and the life and death of Jesus. All these phenomena—as Anders conceives them—share the characteristic of containing an essence within that is accessible through the action of God. This recurring pattern in Anders's way of conceiving the world is what I am calling a disposition. The importance of such a disposition, in this context, is that the believer may discover or sense it through the operation of religious symbols. The believer fastens on a word or an image in the religious language that seems somehow to express something profound, something whose significance extends beyond the reach of articulation. That something is a personal disposition, at once an element of self and a pattern of experience. The fusion of such a disposition with a symbol that allows one to grasp it is a moving experience that is regarded as a manifestation of grace. Like the physical manifestations that mark Per's or Elisabet's religious life, the symbolization of a disposition is an aspect of religious experience that exists beyond the mind, and for that reason is valued by the believer as a unique testimony to the efficacy of God in his or her life.

The existence and import of such experiences can be demonstrated in the faith of other believers. Consider, for example, Kristina, a young, unmarried economics student who is active in various leftist political groups. In fact, Kristina insists that her political outlook is even more basic than her religious views:

> I feel that my political engagement and my analysis of the world around me—which is based on *political* analysis—has to be the starting point for how I can meet God, for how I can see that it [religion] has relevance for my reality....

This is Kristina's side of the story, although I suspect that the fervor of her political engagement owes something to values that she absorbed in her religious upbringing. She conceded this herself through her statement that for her the figure of Jesus is in some way a point of conjunction of the religious and the political:

> My political attitude...says that it is the mass of people that is essential, it's the little person and the struggle (*kampen*) against injustice, the struggle for the little person's right to life. Based on that I can see the picture of Jesus as the picture of a God who puts himself in total solidarity with us. Puts himself on our side, takes part in the struggle (*kampen*), you know what I mean? So it's *not* what the church has said— God with a purple mantle and a gold throne—but a God who comes down where people are most poor, where people are most oppressed, where people are most exposed.

One recognizes immediately the tendency, which she shares with

Anders, for Kristina to assume that God or Jesus is to be found in configurations of events in this world. In Kristina's faith, the assumption is that God is found among the downtrodden and powerless. This conviction articulates neatly with her political views. As a Marxist, Kristina believes that there is a unique power among the working class, among the oppressed, a power that makes their eventual political ascendancy inevitable. Thus, she shares with all Marxist thought the paradoxical conviction that in the long run the truth, political dominance, and utopia—the ultimate powers—are the sole possession of the powerless.

It turns out that Kristina has a similar conception of divine power, for her personal religious philosophy is organized in large part by the drive to purge the stern father figure from what is, after all, a rather authoritarian religion. Thus she speaks repeatedly in the interview of her views as contrasted to those of "the priests." One of the most telling passages occurs when Kristina is talking about what appears to be something else, the classic theodical problem of reconciling the existence of evil with an omnipotent God. She offers a simple if rather unusual solution[4]:

> The only reasonable interpretation I've come up with is that God isn't omnipotent. . . . If he was omnipotent, then he'd just fix it all for us. Oh, sure, they've got all these good and holy logical reasons why he wouldn't do it even if he could. But I can't quite buy it, especially when people start maintaining that he's going to condemn us because he hasn't fixed it.

Kristina goes on to suggest that perhaps the way God works in the world is not "from above," as we are used to thinking about God doing, but in a sense from below, "more like it was a person." I think what she means to suggest is that the concept of omnipotence contradicts her idea of a God who, as she said earlier, is in solidarity with the oppressed. In order for her to respect God, he cannot be one of the powerful but rather, by his very nature, must have limited power.

Kristina's political and religious views are intertwined and in some sense grounded in the same assumption, that there is a power, generated from below, that will always work against authority and for regeneration. Although used in a different way, this is precisely the same proposition as the one which is so important to Anders. God's power is embedded within certain worldly situations, and it appears in the world via a miraculous and unspecifiable process of emergence.

As one might expect on the basis of her political interests, Kristina is articulate on questions of ideals; in particular, she has a clear vision of what a person should get out of life. Recall that Anders, when asked about Jesus' most important message to humanity, referred to his concern with helping persons develop their unique talents. Kristina's reply to a very similar question strikes the same themes:

Interviewer: What do you think Jesus would say is the most important thing for his followers to devote themselves to?
Kristina: To make it possible for people to live a whole life.
Interviewer: What's a whole life?
Kristina: A whole life is when a person has the right, or rather the possibility to take charge of their abilities, their possibilities. I'm getting a little far out now. But the riches that every person has, right? We've got the right to be creative above all.

Kristina believes, as does Anders, that the development of the creativity and talents of the individual is a process of sacred import. The key word "possibilities" here suggests that such development is a manifestation of grace, and this interpretation is strengthened by the observation that it is Jesus himself, in Kristina's view, who endorses such development. Kristina and Anders are agreed that it is in the process of personal transformation that believers are most likely to encounter grace.

Of course, Kristina and Anders would disagree on many, or most, issues they chose to discuss. One is a liberal, the other a communist, and their positions on a wide variety of questions are presumably antithetical. At some level, however, it has been shown that there are some basic values and assumptions that are shared by these believers as well.[5] Each looks to situations of this world as the conveyers of a miraculous power and trusts in the free development of the individual as a road to utopia. Both assume an analytic attitude, an assiduous involvement in group politics, and a profound respect for individuality.[6]

One can certainly see, in other words, how Kristina and Anders can belong to the same church. In spite of their differences, they see grace as being manifested in similar ways. And as I have pointed out for other believers, there is a discernible style to Kristina's thought, a style that creates patterns in disparate areas of concern such as political conviction and religious faith.

As is the case for Anders, this style in Kristina's thought is symbolized for her, summed up from time to time in her daily life, in experiences she regards as profound. For Kristina it is above all in moments of interaction with others, when she is working with others successfully toward a common goal, that she senses that combination of God's presence and personal fulfillment that marks the experience of grace. Asked whether she ever experiences a moment of God's Kingdom here in this world, she responds, "If I have a vision of God's Kingdom, one thing I'm sure of is that a person is *whole* there." The interviewer then asks, "in what situation would that actually happen?" and Kristina answers:

It can happen when you feel *understanding*. When you feel that you're really together, *we,* several people who have the same vision. Creating together on something, so that we are *in* something in some way, right? ... We are together, we want the same thing, and we know, and we know that we are doing it together, we are striving for it together and I am whole, myself, right? At the same time as I am whole with the others.

As with the believers I will discuss in the following chapter, Kristina's experience of grace is characterized not only by the presence of God but by a meaningful interaction with other people as well. Beyond this, such an experience can also be seen to encapsulate the central themes of Kristina's religious thought in general: the stress on solidarity, on discovery of potentiality, on the appearance of divinity in the midst of struggle.

Some believers, like Per and Elisabet, undergo overtly physical experiences that in effect convert[7] themes of thought to somatic symbols. Per, for example, had a conversion that he experienced as a transformation of self. This transformation was as much physical as it was mental. For Anders and Kristina, the physical aspects of the "summarizing" experience are less overt but not necessarily for that reason less meaningful. The physical side of such experiences may take the guise of a feeling of empowerment or strength or conviction; such a feeling is not any less significant for being more diffused in these latter cases.

I will turn now to a third believer, a man whose faith sounds one more variation on the fundamental theme I am developing here. This man, whom I will call Nils, is a recently ordained pastor in SMF (although he has not yet been called to a post). He is 27 years old and newly married. Nils is typical of a large number of younger church members who feel that in the days of their parents the church was overly concerned with cataloging and avoiding a detailed list of worldly sins: dancing, drinking, playing cards, and so on. For Nils, this is not at all what religion is about. For him, sin is the exploitation of the disadvantaged that he perceives occurring in the world around him. Thus, the church activities that he is involved in are discussion and action groups organized around questions of domestic and, particularly, international politics.

Nils feels that a genuine Christian faith will find its expression in a stand against the reigning economic order. In his words:

> In principle... the economic system in our society functions destructively. It represents a lot of what is evil.... Thus one should be able to say, at least on a theoretical level, that the political idea that stands behind this [economic system] must be incompatible with a Christian lifestyle. I mean, the completely developed free market economy... builds in principle on marginalizing people (*utslagning*), that those who don't make it are eliminated. And... to the extent we support this economic system, we support that which is brutal and competitive, and make sure that it will continue.

As might be expected, this attitude also influences Nils's conception of biblical interpretation, which he stresses must lead one to act on the environment:

> I think that the point with faith and so on, the reason I try to maintain it and live by it... it's all, the Bible and everything, a way to influence (*bearbeta*) existence, our whole existence, the things that happen around me.

In talking about the sermon Nils extends this point, saying that the only way a Bible text becomes meaningful is through applying it to experience:

> I think that if it [the sermon] is going to be meaningful, then you've got to consciously deal with this connection (*koppling*) the whole time, so that if you take up a Bible text, then... you've got to make the connection: what does this mean for me? In the relations where I find myself and so on, among the everyday stories that I have all around me.

Unlike Per, for example, Nils stresses that biblical interpretation is a creative act. At one point he says the Word of the Bible is like the blind in a window, the point is to try to see the light behind the lines. One does not just read the Word and know what it means; one must work to understand it. This points to another difference between these two men. In contrast to Per, who insists that the Word can only be comprehended by "acting it out" in experience, Nils conceives of interpretation as a comparison and subsequent application to experience. The former understands the Word in applying it, the latter understands and *then* applies it.

As Per was characterized by his "closeness" to the religious symbol, Nils can be said to illustrate a consistent distance in respect to the Word. An interpretation is always interposed between Nils and the religious symbol, connecting him to the symbol but at the same time separating him from it. Consider the way Nils looks at a particular Bible passage, a parable.

In this parable, which is taken from the Book of Matthew (Chapter 25: 14 – 30), a master gives three servants various quantities of gold and then leaves on a long journey. When he returns, two of the servants have invested their gold and doubled the quantity, while the third, frightened of losing it, has simply buried his gold. The master praises the first two servants and chastises the third. Nils interprets this parable by equating the master with God and the gold with the different talents and innate goodness he ostensibly gives each of us. Nils concludes from the parable that our talents belong in circulation, in service to others, not bottled up within the individuals that possess them:

> In every person there exists something good, an ability to develop something positive in relation to other people and to society as a whole.... But I believe that these possibilities are not given to people if they are always just sitting on the sidelines.

This statement has obvious affinities to the positions on "the possibilities of development" expressed by Anders and Kristina. Like those two believers, Nils stresses that grace, a gift of God, makes possible the process of development and transformation of the self; also similar to Anders and (particularly) Kristina is Nils's insistence that such development must serve social, not selfish, ends.

One can certainly see how the linkage between grace and personal development has occurred. It has been shown how a disposition regarding symbols—objects of thought—comes to permeate and characterize that thought, and, in particular, how such a disposition comes to constitute a virtual framework for the self. It is the consistency born of the workings of such dispositions that enables believers, when reflecting on their experience, to sense or at times explicitly recognize a pattern that coheres in their experience and thus characterizes them. Such recognition, however, is dependent upon a symbolic process. The only way a disposition can become available to thought is by being symbolized. If that symbolization is effected by any Christian symbol, the process itself comes to reinforce the truth of the fundamental Christian message: something which is beyond experience may enter into experience and become a part of this world. Grace, the story of Jesus Christ, and the process of self-transformation partake of the same basic logic.

In this conjunction of divinity and self lie the "possibilities" of faith in SMF; as the minister wrote, "God's grace is actually Christ and his presence entails a possibility to find oneself and one's purpose." It is as if the age-old manifestation of "amazing grace" in the evangelical tradition, the personal conversion, had been extended over time and made an ongoing process rather than a one-time transformation.

Jesus Christ is of course the quintessential symbol of the process of God's grace, and thus it is interesting to note that Christ is also—half man, half God—a conjunction of divinity and a self. As has been demonstrated in previous examples, this equivalence often occurs in personal faiths as the identification of grace, as it appears in the believer's life, and Christ. Nils's faith provides yet another example. It has been noted that he stresses the importance of a creative interpretation in mediating God's Word to the believer. When asked, "What was the most important thing about the coming of Jesus?," he responds:

> I think maybe the most important thing with Jesus coming to earth and so on is precisely that—simply that he did come to earth. If you see Jesus as God's son in one way or another, the important thing is just that he did that. And likewise, that has to do with the stuff I said earlier about there being a connection between the Christian faith and my everyday situation.

The important thing about Jesus is that he, precisely like the interpretation, mediates between God and earth. He is in fact the human, physical, manifestation of Nils's approach to the symbols of his faith: the significance is in the interpretation, the personal version of the abstract or general. This conviction extends to the way Nils thinks about life in general, for he believes that his purpose in life is to offer something of *himself* to others, something that transcends abstract social principle and utilizes that which is unique to him. Asked, "What is it to make something of life?" he replies:

> To engage yourself with others. It's hard to get away from, even though it's sort of a cliché, this thing about playing roles, that there are so many expectations in society in general, in our congregations, in our meetings, that you should act in a particular way and so on. To try and get away from that, to try anyway to be what you really are.

In this passage, at once an echo of the individualism of Anders and Kristina and a statement of political commitment, one gets a glimpse of what is most important to Nils: to transcend the structures of authority, of society, of expectation, and to offer a bit of the unique self to one's fellows. These comprise the emotional center of his faith. Not surprisingly, he sees Jesus as acting in the same way:

> You can...see [in the Bible] how Jesus stood up for what he said and how controversial he was. If you look at it this way, you realize it couldn't have ended differently than it did. He made himself impossible. They were forced to move him out of the way. He subverted the whole religious authority, everything the society was built on....He went into the places where you don't ask questions and asked questions and attacked the religious authorities.

In one sense, it is a long way from Per's personal conversion to Nils's political engagement. But the examples I have drawn upon in this chapter are intended to demonstrate that, in another sense, the two forms of experience are fundamentally similar. Each of these phenomena encapsulates on an experiential level the dispositions that characterize believers' thought in other spheres. Whether it manifests itself as the physical effervescence of human interaction, a diffuse feeling of empowerment, or a moment of self-transformation, the experience of living one's faith strengthens the believer's commitment to the symbols of his or her faith.

This final statement should not be read as a truism but rather interpreted in light of the special emphasis I have placed on the concept of commitment. Commitment is a fusion of self and religious symbol, it is a relation in which the believer's *identity* is constituted by the symbol. The nature of this identification can be grasped only by an effort of thought which dissolves the conventional categories of body and mind; identification, and hence commitment, occur beyond intention and beyond thought.

The critic Kenneth Burke (1973: 9) once referred to the symbolic act as "the dancing of an attitude." Similarly, I would refer to the experience in which a believer feels his or her faith as "living out a commitment." But such an activity occurs not in the debased sense of following a rule; I am not referring to the phenomenon of action in accord with an abstract principle sincerely held. People do, at least at times, act in accord with their principles, but here I wish to point to something completely different. In the profound experience that encapsulates faith the believer *is* the symbol, the symbol is thus incarnated in the social world. Such experiences are but the radical manifestation of the general process of commitment, which is the tendency to appropriate the symbols of faith as constituents of the self.

6

⚜

Grace and the
Foundation of Experience

In this, the final chapter in which I
discuss the faiths of individual believers, I will turn to one further variation
on the theme that the process of grace is involved in the creation and maintenance of the self. In a way the examples I will cite here are the most striking
of those I have discussed, as well as being among the most commonly
encountered. Whereas believers like those described in the previous chapter
state that God helps people realize their true or potential selves, the believers
I will now introduce take a more radical position: Without grace it is not
possible to *be* a self or to function as a person should in the social world. The
following examples show very clearly how grace can be conceived as providing a necessary component of the self, creating capacities without which it
cannot properly exist.

As I have been careful to stress throughout this work, however, such an
idea should not be seen as an element of a consensual culture in the congregation. Rather, the common conception that grace somehow completes
the self is an idea, more or less articulable, that is constantly reinforced and
rediscovered in social intercourse at the church as well as in the experience of
individual believers. Some readers will ask, "but isn't a shared idea more
than this?" "How," they might continue, "does it happen that the believers at
Immanuel Church all share this conception rather than some other one, or
indeed that they share any idea at all? Without the notion of a consensual

culture, it seems that one must reduce shared ideas to the mysteriously congruent ideas of individual believers."

To such a reader I would answer that it is those who advocate "culture as consensus" who appeal to mysterious, albeit by now widely accepted, processes. In the end, the assertion that an autonomous level of culture somehow exists and somehow imposes itself on persons does nothing to help us understand congruent ideas in a community. In fact, such an assertion effectively precludes the investigation of the actual processes whereby consensus emerges by pretending these processes need no explanation.

In recent years the culture-as-consensus position has been forcefully and often convincingly expressed by the anthropologist Clifford Geertz. Geertz's position is evident in his oft-repeated claim that meaning is "public" (see, for example, 1973: 12), by which he means that cultural forms are associated with a shared and commonly accessible level of meanings. As has been shown, such a position has a long tradition in anthropological thought, but in Geertz's writing it is buttressed by his reading of twentiety-century philosophy. Since modern views of semantics reject "privacy" theories of meaning, Geertz implies, they must accept a "publicity" theory of meaning such as the one he offers.

Although this argument is gracefully made, it is incorrect. In the first place, the rejection of traditional "meanings in the head" semantics does not imply the acceptance of an equally simple "meanings out there" position; the problem of meanings in language remains something of a mystery, as the ongoing debate among philosophers demonstrates.[1] Second, the fact that we use the word "meaning" to refer to processes whereby people understand both words and complex ideological symbols does not justify the conclusion that the processes of linguistic and ideological understanding are the same or even analogous.

Thus, I cannot agree with Geertz that the meaning of, say, religious symbols is public. It is precisely because meaning in the large sense is *not* a public process that people all over the world strive to create, discover, and reinforce common meanings. Consensus is the accomplishment of a community; community is not the accomplishment of consensus. It is because finding meaning is not a public process that potentially meaningful collective events assume such significance in communal life. In such events the person has the opportunity to feel solidarity with his or her neighbors, and perhaps to conceive common meanings that may for a time endure. But to deduce from people's yearning for and achievement of common meanings the *a priori* existence of common meanings—as the position that meanings are "public" does—is to skip directly over the point. People struggle to create and to locate their togetherness, and the problem for any investigator of the role of cultural systems in social life is to discover how they do this.

To reconceive culture as commitment is to undertake such a task. To do so is to abandon the convenient but sterile notion that culture floats above the mind, ruling it, for the inconvenient but fertile understanding that culture is to a significant extent appropriated *below* the mind, as the commitments that constitute the self. Members of the community are thus able to discover meanings in their lives that are conditioned by the order inherent in cultural systems, but this does not mean that those meanings are available to be plucked, ripe and ready for consumption, from the Edenic cultural tree.

As noted, the examples to be considered below contain some strong evidence for this perspective on the operation of culture, that is, for seeing culture as operating below the mind, in the physical processes that underlie thought. This is clearly illustrated in the words of a believer I will call Maryann; she is single, near the age of retirement, and works as a hospital adminstrator. Although intelligent and engaged in an active social life, Maryann is at the same time frustrated with certain aspects of her life, perhaps most obviously by what she sees as her inability to express herself. She asked to stop her interview twice and complained again and again of the difficulty of formulating her thoughts. The following exchange is typical:

> *Maryann:* How is this poor American going to get anything out of this, with my difficulties in expressing what I mean?
> *Interviewer:* I don't know, but you've got an unlimited palette, you can paint a picture of the church as you see it.[2]
> *Maryann:* But I don't have a palette, that's what I'm saying, I don't have any ability.
> *Interviewer:* But you are so full of thoughts and longing.
> *Maryann:* Yes, but I can't *say* it. It's like I didn't get the instrument that makes people able to talk, to formulate things.

Continuing, Maryann traces this difficulty to her upbringing as a woman:

> [It's because] if you're a woman you're oppressed. . . . You know they say if women politicians say something they've got to say it twice as well as a man, and they often do. And so lots of times I haven't said things in situations where I've felt I should. Sometimes I've wanted to say something in church, for example, but I've held my tongue, and then somebody else has said the same thing and it's been really well received. This kind of thing is such a big problem.

Maryann gives another hint as to the nature of her frustration at her perceived inability to articulate her faith in the following lines:

> I don't know, sometimes people say, "What a Bible verse that is, it's so strong for me." And it's that kind of thing I can never talk about, because I can never capture what I experience.

There is an ambiguity here; does Maryann mean she cannot capture what she experiences in reading a Bible verse or what she experiences in a life situation where she applies such a verse? In fact, I think her formulation refers to both at once. What Maryann finds difficult to capture in words is the relationship between scripture and experience. She feels inadequate compared with those who can offer a coherent exegesis of Bible verses and their impact in their lives.

To speak is not the only problem with which Maryann is concerned. Two similar verbs, "to see" *(att se)* and "to hear" *(att höra)* (or "to listen", *att lyssna)* are also important to her, and these terms come up again and again as Maryann discusses her faith. She first mentions "listening" to explain what she hopes to gain from prayer:

> If I pray for another person then I pray at the same time that I understand how I can help. Either because I have arms and legs and can walk[3] [i.e., she is not handicapped, as are some of her friends] or so that I can listen or best of all give something of value.

To hear and see another person is, for Maryann, to notice, to care about her. Both these words, although the most common of "everyday" verbs, have biblical overtones for Maryann:

> There's something in the Old Testament, in a Psalm, that occurs to me here, that we see one another. . . . This "your eyes saw me" is something I think I understand. Because I experience that so often, when I am doing something with people, that they don't see me. I'm thinking of a pastor who doesn't see me. . . .

Like Per, Maryann has a thorough understanding of scripture, and the Word can be shown to pervade her speech in rather subtle ways.[4] Her conceptualizations of problems in her life are often rooted in biblical imagery, and the terms she uses here are a good example of this. Since references to seeing, hearing, and speaking are fairly common in the Old Testament, it is not possible to specify exactly what passages she is calling on here. However, the general idea of such passages can be safely assumed to be similar to the following passage, which occurs in the fifteenth Psalm and is repeated almost exactly (except for the deletion of the seventh verse) in Psalm 135:

> [4]Their idols are silver and gold,
> made by the hands of men.
>
> [5]They have mouths that cannot speak
> and eyes that cannot see;
>
> [6]they have ears that cannot hear,
> nostrils and cannot smell;
>
> [7]with their hands they cannot feel,
> with their feet they cannot walk,

and no sound comes from their throats.

⁸Their makers grow to be like them,
and so do all who trust in them. (New English Bible)

Compare this passage with Jeremiah 5: 21: "Listen, you foolish and senseless people, who have eyes and see nothing, ears and hear nothing." The exact reference that Maryann is drawing upon is in any case not particularly important; what is significant here is the image of sensory incapacity that is used to express separation from God. In Maryann's usage, such incapacity is further identified with an inability or unwillingness to render service or even attention to those in need. To take the care to listen and to see, on the other hand, is to use one's possibilities, to do God's work:

When we know what possibilities we'd have if we were really open, if we . . . *saw and heard.* You know it says here [in the Bible] that you must *see with the eyes and hear although you don't hear.* . . . I like those words. . . . When you believe that you can get help from the one who has created all this, who has created me and given me all these possibilities *to be able to listen* in some way and *to be able to see,* then I think you can say that a person is a possibility. . . . I am a resource, God needs you and me. If he didn't have us, well, he just couldn't get by without us *(han klarar sig inte utan oss)* in certain situations. (my emphasis)

The first thing to point out here is that Maryann connects the program of seeing and hearing to the "possibilities" given by God. Furthermore, God is actually working *through* the person who sees and hears, God *needs* such people to do his work. The references to "possibilities" suggest that Maryann is discussing her ideas about grace here, for "possibilities" is, as has been noted, a common term for grace in the church. It is also easy to see that, as she discusses grace in terms of functioning senses, Maryann uses sensory incapacity as an analogy for evil. As in the Psalm, the bad things in her life arise from her or others' inability to see, hear, or speak. This analogy has a direct and intriguing implication: evil is construed here as the blockage of the most important tools for contacting experience. Evil is described as the inaccessibility of experience.

Here, then, is yet another variation on the familiar theme. Grace is conceived in the idiom of physical sensation and of speech, and its absence as sensory incapacity. Maryann's religion is not a mental outlook or a series of propositions to which she assents as much as it is a way of seeing or of hearing. Her faith is imprinted in her sensory capacities.

As the passage makes clear, these capacities are the conduit through which flows, in one direction, the energy of God, in the other, the needs of other human beings. Thus, in Maryann's case, the feeling of energy or empowerment that has been shown to be associated with the experience of grace takes the form of the joy of empathizing with and helping others. This "joy of human contact" is a possibility available to Maryann because she can speak, hear, and see, capacities given to her by God so that she might do his work.

In this sense, an important part of Maryann's self, in essence that part which enables her to interrelate sensitively with others, is given by God. God in a sense *completes* Maryann's self. These two features—first, that God completes the self and second that he does so in a way that enables one to interact closely with others—are present to some extent in a good number of the interviews conducted in this study. Consider, for example, a 27-year-old physical therapist named Lena. Lena is an articulate and emotional woman, who conceives her life as something of a struggle to preserve that which is meaningful and valuable in the face of forces all around her in life that would tend to destroy those values. These forces of destruction impinge on her constantly; in fact, Lena stresses that even much of what she observes at Immanuel Church fits into this category:

> *Lena:* What you should get out of a church service is sort of a self-renewal, relaxation. But sometimes I feel like it's really hard to go there. I feel all this narrow-mindedness *(inskränktheten)*. I think the church fosters a lot of "perfect people." Perfect thinking, career oriented, sometimes it's so far from Jesus. It's so far from this idea of "come as you are." There have been Sundays where I've gone home and had to struggle so hard that the tears run down and I've thought: I don't want to be a member in that kind of a church, I don't want to be a member where you're supposed to be so perfect. I'm scared I might start to think that way too if I keep going there.
> *Interviewer:* What is so perfect, do you think? . . .
> *Lena:* The worship service is so perfect, the language is so perfect, and the people are so well-adjusted *(anpassad)* that they look alike, they have the same kind of clothes. Sometimes I sense this feeling like "I'm good because I'm good to use for this or that." I'm not good just because I'm a person, or good because I'm [Lena].

Lena goes on to talk about how only the most talented individuals sing solos and read and preach in Immanuel Church, and thus how everyone else, the "normal" people, are left feeling awed by the service but not especially good about themselves. Bluntly put, Lena dislikes the worship service at her church. She feels it works directly against a central message of Christianity, that one's self-worth is a result of one's personhood and relationship to God, not of one's talents and accomplishments.

In this sense, the worship service acts in a manner opposed to its ostensible end, contact with God, and in fact could be said to fit into Lena's conception of what is evil:

> Evil is all that which hinders us from getting contact with God. I don't believe that it's a person [i.e., evil is not a personified "devil" for Lena] who fights and, so to speak, corresponds to a divine force. I mean, all

those things that stand between God and us; I believe that a lot of those things in existence are things we ourselves have produced. Things that make us create distance. There are so many, it's so enormously easy to fall into something that creates distance from God. It can be one's own narrow-mindedness *(inskränkthet)* when something else becomes extremely important. . . .

The worship service, in its pursuit of perfection, can draw people's attention to excellence and accomplishment, and hence distract them from God. (Recall that Lena characterized the "perfect" people in the church as "narrow-minded," and here she cites this as something that creates distance from God, something evil.) Her vision of what a church and a worship service *should* provide is "enough support so that you can have the strength to function sensibly in the everyday world." A latent contrast can thus be drawn out of Lena's words: Evil, that which creates distance from God and other people, is a narrowing, a concentrating on the false. God is support, support to "function sensibly."

What does Lena mean by support, or by functioning sensibly? Her further comments suggest the beginnings of an answer:

[A church service should help us be] this salt and light.[5] To make us uncomfortable. To make us stand for human values and so on, every day, like I did when I went to the dramatic institute last year. Every *day* was a struggle *(kamp)*. Every single day I had to stand up for my values. Because I have completely different values than, well I think 92 percent of their values were of a certain type. So I had to stand up for my values which said that all people have a human worth. I didn't ever want to fall into this disdaining other people just because they didn't think like I do. That was a struggle *(kamp)* I had to be equipped *(var rustad)* for every single day. It was so hard it was crazy. If I hadn't had my friends in church who understood this, who supported *(stödje)* me, I wouldn't have gotten through *(hade inte klarat av)* that year. And now I feel a lot stronger afterwards . . . so during that period I was going to services, struggling with my faith. And it [the worship service] was so foreign to our reality, if they hadn't said the services dealt with this struggle, I would've missed it. It's so foreign from what it is today. I feel like the church is so far away from me, from our working life and from our environment. Just like there simply wasn't a struggle. They could have questioned some people who think it's a struggle to be a person, a struggle to be a Christian today. And let them *tell about* that in the service, because that could have been strong to use. But instead they just stand there and slap together a bunch of sentences.

Lena says that the support she needed at a difficult time in her life was provided by her friends, and the description she gives of what should go on in church reveals her conviction that a church service should function in much the same way. The church service should talk about the problems believers encounter in their lives, as close friends do. With such support people can function sensibly, can reach their goal of "being persons" with human values.

Lena describes her hard times at the dramatic institute as "a struggle . . . to stand up for my values." To live according to human values is a problem of which she is ever aware, and the problem to which she feels the church should address itself. Although Lena does not state what she means by "human values," my experience in the church allows me to offer a probably accurate guess. She refers to a complex of qualities that center around cooperation and creativity. Compassion, admission of vulnerability, and self-expression are "human values"; divisiveness, competition, and any emotion (for example, pride) that hampers free expression are not. As an American, I was often subjected (both by church members and others) to short lectures on the silliness of what my friends took to be an American ideal: the strong and isolated individual who could *klara sig själv*, make it by himself. The rugged individualism of American frontier mythology is close to the opposite of what Lena means by "human values."

To be a person is to be true to one's self and to acknowledge the importance of one's fellow persons in pursuing that goal. Lena often uses a phrase, *jag klarar det har inte själv*—I can't handle this (or "make it") by myself—that exemplifies this philosophy. To think that one can proceed through difficulties solely on the basis of individual strengths (a delusion to which I, as an American, was thought especially prone) is to deny the vital social aspect of existence. All humans need the strength and support offered by other people, exactly as Lena did during her difficult days at the dramatic institute.

As was shown above, Lena holds that a worship service should work to provide the kind of "support" she gets from her friends. It turns out that this kind of support is what Jesus offers her as well:

> I place him [Jesus] beside me, especially when I'm working with some really difficult group at work. [Lena is a rehabilitative therapist in a hospital.] *When I feel I can't manage this myself (jag klarar det här inte-själv)*, it's too much for me, too much of a responsibility to be able to give some person something. Then I sometimes say, aloud right there in the room, "Come now, Jesus, and we'll go and do a good job." I mean, prayer for me isn't something where you sit down so seriously and pray. For me it's just an everyday thing. So I think that all of life is a prayer because *I can't get through it by myself (jag klarar mig inte själv)*. (my emphasis)

The repeated use of this phrase, "I can't handle this by my*self*," points to a particular kind of insufficiency that is ameliorated by Jesus, an insufficiency of self. Lena reports that Jesus gives her what the worship service *should* give her, the kind of support she gets from her closest friends. Like Maryann, Lena finds the center of her faith in an experience of completion of the self.

Furthermore, the effect of this experience is to enable her to make it through a difficult social situation, where others need her, where she would otherwise feel insufficient to handle the situation. Once again, the believer holds that God completes the self in such a way as to enable the believer to function socially, to do God's work among others.

If it is true that believers often feel their faith in an experience of commitment that completes or fulfills the self, one might expect that a believer *unhappy* with her faith might articulate her dissatisfaction in terms of "something missing," something incomplete in her physical makeup. One interview conducted in this study clearly fulfills this expectation.

Anna is a woman in her mid-thirties who works as a secretary. When she was younger she studied a foreign language at the university but dropped out before receiving her degree. Anna was one of the relatively few people we interviewed who seemed not only doubtful about their faith, but troubled by that doubt:

> I think that faith, which [has at times been] . . . a source of *security* within me, it feels real foggy just now. I'm afraid, somewhere I'm afraid that the little faith I have, that it will disappear. Leave me standing in *complete emptiness*. (my emphasis)

This "fogginess" is based less on any doubt that God exists than on a feeling that he is not entering in any significant way into Anna's life, is not, as she expresses it, leading her:

> We talk so much about leading, maybe I've gotten it on the brain. But I sure don't feel it right now. I feel like I'm standing in a *big empty room*. I don't know what I should do. (my emphasis)

At other times, Anna has experienced such "leading," a feeling that things in her life were working and that difficulties were working themselves out. For example, when she moved to Stockholm five years ago, she needed a place to live, and one day an acquaintance just walked up and asked her if she wanted to take the apartment she now lives in. Anna saw the hand of God in this coincidence. Leading, that is, is a metaphor—based on the experience of movement—that refers to an ostensible divine involvement in Anna's action.

At the time Anna's interview was conducted, such leading—and the sense of security it brings—was missing from her life. Time and again she expressed this situation in terms of sensory blurriness, emptiness, and an inability to contact the world that surrounds her. Her faith is "fuzzy" or "foggy," she feels suspended "in the empty air":

> Just now I'm in one of these *empty* periods where I don't pray. But maybe that's a result of it [her faith] being so fuzzy. I think it feels like I don't have any answers, like *I'm in the empty air*. But in the time when I

did pray, I think I prayed a lot to be used, to get to mean something. . . .
I miss it, but maybe it's also connected with this *security*, maybe it was
that too, that it gave me *security* to pray. (my emphasis)

Not only is there something missing in Anna's life, there is something
missing in *her*. She feels *empty*, and emptiness surrounds her.[6] Specifically,
what is missing above all are those capacities in which Maryann and Lena
located their commitment, the abilities to relate to others. Anna reaches out
and cannot find anything to touch. It is precisely the capacities that Maryann
named, the ability to see and hear others, that Anna cites as characteristic of
the time when her faith was functioning:

I think that when it was working [her faith], I think that *I saw people* all
around who I, I don't know, but I sort of thought that it was God who
worked with me, *I saw people, I saw what they needed.* I thought that *I
saw people,* I can't explain it any other way. That *I listened to them.* (my
emphasis)

Reading Anna's words, one cannot help but be struck by the remarkable
similarity of this metaphor to the one used by Maryann. Note, however, that
Anna is not repeating a stock formulation, but rather ("I can't explain it any
other way") she is reaching to express something solidly rooted in her
physical experience. Indeed, the obscurity of this metaphor is such that—
where it not for the availability of Maryann's more extensive use of the same
comparison—it would probably remain opaque to an outside observer.

The parallel between these expressions, in short, is in all likelihood
rooted *not* in the widespread occurrence of the metaphor of seeing and
hearing. Rather, a physical awareness of faith, a disposition shared by Anna
and Maryann, finds similar expression in words. Maryann and Anna use the
same words, but here it seems to be an *experience,* a commitment, that they
share, and not a common outlook impressed upon them by the authority of
the metaphors they use.

This observation has relevance for the understanding of all the
believers discussed in the preceding chapters. The relationships between
faith and experience described here are not a simple matter of symbols whose
consensual meanings shape the outlooks of believers who use them. The
symbols of faith, to be sure, shape experience, but their most important
contribution in this process is best conceived as pre-linguistic. It is in the
experience of commitment to a symbol, an identification that often takes the
form of an explicitly physical merging of an image of faith and the image of
self, that the influence of this religion takes shape.

In chapter four, commitment took the form of ecstatic experiences that
give believers a sense of communion with God while at the same time
providing emotional support or allowing the self to readapt to its environment. In the next chapter, several believers were introduced who speak of a

less ecstatic but continuous process of self-transformation, a process in which they find a profound meaning. But in both of these forms of religious experience, similar component processes can be observed. In both forms, believers' thought was shown to be in part organized by certain elemental dispositions such as "volitional transcendence" or "emergence." Such dispositions, which impart order to believers' experience, come to be associated with the action of divinity, presumably through a process in which the believer locates the symbols—from among the countless available Christian images—which seem to have a peculiar salience for him or her. However this equivalence arises, its effect is that, on the one hand, those religious symbols whose imagery can be adapted to the disposition assume a mysterious profundity for the believer. On the other hand, the believer's identity or self, in being blended with certain elements of the religious language, may be shaped by those elements.

In this chapter, believers have been described who associate divinity directly with the very accessibility of experience. For these persons, the self is simply incomplete without the presence of divinity. Again, elemental dispositions are linked to an appropriate religious symbol or set of symbols, with the result that symbol and disposition reinforce one another. I have called this relationship one of identification: the symbol is meaningful because it represents the disposition, the disposition is accessible to consciousness because it may be formulated in terms of the symbol. Thus, for example, religious imagery enabled all of the women described in this chapter to articulate and, more important, enabled two of them to find help in dealing with pervasive difficulties generated in the course of their lives.

In the following, concluding, chapter I will discuss the implications of these findings for the study of groups like SMF, as well as for the question of how culture works in ordering social life. In addition, I will retrace a few of the themes of earlier chapters and consider what they might tell us about life in Immanuel Church and in Sweden as a whole.

7

The Image of Salvation

> Religious phenomena are naturally arranged in two fundamental catego-
> ries: beliefs and rites. The first are states of opinion, and consist in
> representations; the second are determined modes of action. Between
> these two classes of facts there is all the difference which separates
> thought from action. (Durkheim 1915: 51)

This passage, written in the early twentieth century by Emile Durkheim, reflects a distinction that was central to social scientific thought about
religion at that time. In more recent years it has come to be widely accepted
that not only the distinction but the very terms in which it is formulated are
not the most fruitful ones for social scientific analysis. Belief, in particular,
has more or less dropped out of the theoretical lexicon of sociology and
anthropology, replaced by "symbols" and "meaning systems," terms that
avoid the mentalistic connotations of belief. Although "ritual" remains a
widely used term, it is fair to say that interest has shifted away from ritual as
a circumscribed sphere of "especially religious" action and toward the influence of religion on action as a whole.

In sum, it has been accepted that the significant problem for research in
the field of religion is not the separation between belief and rite but rather
the *interplay* between symbol and action. In Clifford Geertz's (1973: 90)
seminal formulation, the important problem is how religion "tunes human
actions to an envisaged cosmic order and projects images of cosmic order
onto the plane of human experience."

. The analysis I have offered in the previous chapters has been intended not to contradict this position but to extend it. Specifically, I want to suggest that the language of "mutual influence" between symbol and action is, for certain situations, still too close to the old division of belief and ritual. For if one speaks of "mutual influence" between two levels, one has necessarily accepted the validity of their separation. In the case of the believers I studied, however, it may be most appropriate to do away with the distinction altogether. The notion of commitment is intended to accomplish this purpose, to mediate the received distinction between belief and ritual, between thought and action. Although I introduced the idea of commitment as a peculiarly strong belief, I could have just as accurately—although not, I think, as comprehensibly—introduced it as a peculiarly significant action.

My focus on commitment is an attempt to move beyond the idea that the social efficacy of a symbolic system must stem from the attempts of believers to bring their behavior into congruence with their beliefs. Thought and action meet in commitment in a different way than they do in the process of conforming to a rule. Much of my concern in the previous chapters has been to demonstrate how commitment is a better way to conceive the religious experience of the believers at Immanuel Church than is the assumption that they are seeking to live in accord with beliefs shared throughout the group.

My goal, however, is not only to describe the processes whereby the men and women of Immanuel Church discover meaning and live their religious lives but also to suggest how commitment plays a role in shaping *social* processes in this group. Specifically, I want to address the question of how commitment contributes to social cohesion in the group. In this final chapter, I will turn to this task.

I will approach this question through another puzzle in the realm of consensus, namely, what is the image of salvation at Immanuel Church? Were one to nominate one tenet of belief at Immanuel Church for the status "consensual," a statement to which all members would assent, certainly that statement would be that the one God appeared on earth as Jesus Christ and that this event has a direct significance for believers' lives.[1] In less colorful language, one could say church members are very likely to agree that they are offered salvation through God's grace, a process symbolized in his incarnation. Salvation, then, can be named as the reason they seek grace, the reason they seek—in the various ways demonstrated in previous chapters— to commit themselves.

Salvation, however, is not by any means an easily fathomed topic at Immanuel Church. The now familiar problem once again asserts itself: Members may agree on the symbol's import, but it quickly becomes clear to any observer that this consensus does not extend to the symbol's meaning. Salvation may indicate life after death, the acquiring of a new outlook in the present life, or some other meaningful but mundane experience. Like every other term used by believers at Immanuel Church, salvation seems to be appropriated by believers in idiosyncratic ways.

As with "grace," however, certain patterns are evident in the various uses to which the term salvation is put in the church. In the first place, the word salvation is in fact only rarely used to refer to life after death, and this is quite significant. We may safely assume that When Martin Luther agonized over his state of grace it was precisely the issues of paradise and hell—in short, life after death—that interested him. The image of hell as eternal torment was a real and terrifying one for him[2]; Luther, as Roland Bainton (1950: 25) wrote, "became and monk for exactly the same reason as thousands of others, namely, in order to save his soul." But although life after death is discussed at Immanuel Church, it is anything but an overriding concern. I can recall only one sermon that treated the topic of heaven, and none that discussed hell as a possible fate after death.

The sermon that discussed heaven did so, as is typical of this church, in order to promote a "this-worldly" interpretation of the concept. Believers are consistently urged to concentrate on bringing good into the life they live here on earth; any concern with the afterlife is thought to distract from that task and is often actively discouraged.

This emphasis can be observed in a concept related to salvation, "the kingdom of heaven," or alternatively, "the kingdom of God." These phrases are used repeatedly by Jesus in the gospels in an ambiguous fashion, to refer perhaps to heaven, perhaps to a coming utopia in this world. I often asked believers about this ambiguity: is it true that the kingdom of God may manifest itself on earth? The possibility of a utopia on earth was usually dismissed but, as I have indicated, so was the conception of God's kingdom as life after death:

> I'd like to believe in a kingdom of heaven on the earth. I'd like to believe that you can work for, or that you can be active in a way that will bring about, a kingdom of heaven on the earth. But I just don't believe we'll see a kingdom of heaven on the earth.... And then if there's going to be a kingdom of heaven after death or not, that's something I never devote any thought to. It's never felt important.

Although some believers are undoubtedly more concerned with the issue of life after death than is this young woman, no one we spoke to said more than a few words about the topic. The point is not that most church members do not believe that the promise of eternal life their faith offers is valid but rather that this is not a salient image of salvation for them. Whether or not it is indeed possible to specify something consensual in the meaning of salvation, the promise of eternal life is not the place to begin the search. But are there other possible images of salvation at the church?

The first answer that comes to mind is that grace itself is salvation at Immanuel Church. That is, I have introduced the notion of commitment, a physical-mental process that believers refer to as grace. I have interpreted the reception of grace as a process of self-formation that is experienced by believers as a moment of profound insight and/or emotional salience, a moment or recurring experience when their selves and their world are illuminated. As such, grace would seem to offer sufficient benefits in itself that it might be sought as an end rather than a means to the end of salvation. This, then, is the second possibility that must be considered. If an image of salvation cannot be located, is it not because the experience of grace has been so elaborated in this church that grace itself is salvation, a moment of harmony worth pursuing in its own right? Is it not reasonable to assume that grace and salvation have collapsed into one another, so that grace is its own end?

In order to answer this question it is necessary to ponder just why the process of commitment is so elaborated in this church. The reason must be sought in the historical conditions which produced SMF and, before that, Pietism. As was explained in the second chapter, the essential Pietist innovation was the emphasis on the sole importance of the "inner" relationship to God; the various forms of commitment that have been discussed in subsequent chapters are the ways in which the demand for an inner relationship is met in Immanuel Church. But whence this demand? Why did the early Pietists, and before them that introspective malcontent Martin Luther, posit such a relationship as the channel of God's grace?

Here it is helpful to recall that the early Pietist Francke, like Martin Luther, was a man beset by doubt. Luther's doubt took the form of uncertainty as to his salvation; Francke's doubt took a more basic form, the question of the very authority of the Christian faith. He wrote of his period of doubt: "No longer did I believe any God in heaven, and that was the end of that. I could not hold fast to God's word or to man's word; I found at that time as little power in the one as I did in the other" (Francke 1969 [orig. 1690 – 91]: 26, cited in Meyer 1984: 15).

The certainty of the *inner* relationship between person and God becomes necessary only when *uncertainty* grows to be a formidable threat. The need for the inner relationship to God is born of doubt, of being insufficiently convinced. Thus, if one asks after the source of the essential Protestant tenet that it is the individual, the single person, who stands before God, there is no better answer than to look to the situation of competing ideologies in the late Middle Ages. The Renaissance, the birth of mercantile capitalism, the breakup of the feudal order, the whole of the social process in the fifteenth and sixteenth centuries tended to encourage the differentiation of competing points of view. This is not to say that European society prior to this time had been a monolith, but between medieval and modern forms of society there is after all the profound difference that in the latter one cannot even locate orthodoxy, much less bow to it.

It is the loss of the authority of orthodoxy that demands an inner relationship between the individual and God, for the very reason that the ritual assurances of orthodoxy no longer *convince*. And the experience of grace, formulated in Protestantism and refined in Pietism, was originally the believer's assurance of that relationship, his or her guarantee of salvation.

Thus in a logical, and probably also in a historical sense, the moral individualism and the elaboration of commitment that can be observed in Immanuel Church as much follow from ideological fragmentation as cause it. In much historical and sociological writing, of course, it is assumed that individualism is at the root of ideological fragmentation. It is asserted that the Western world lacks a common culture, that the modern community is fragmented *because of* deeply entrenched individualism. By now there may be a certain amount of truth in this perspective, but it obscures the fundamental social complex of individualism, noncollective ritual, and ideological diversity. For many purposes, it may be more useful to examine the interconnections among these phenomena than to point a finger at one of these levels as the cause of the others.

It certainly makes sense, for example, to view the elaboration of commitment as a response to the tormenting situation of ideological fragmentation, for one important result of the reception of grace is precisely the alleviation of that torment. In the face of the threatening uncertainty not only as to what to believe but what to be, the mechanism of commitment facilitates resolution by validating one alternative. Thus, the authority no longer possessed by any orthodoxy is reconstituted on the level of the experience of commitment.

However, this is not the only result of the commitment relationship. Ritual has always served as the means whereby the authority of dominant ideals was established; from another perspective this same process could be termed the *embodiment* of dominant ideals. But there is another component of ritual, just as universal and just as significant. Ritual is always, in some sense, collective action.

To this point in the discussion I have referred to the form of ritual observed at Immanuel Church as personal ritual in order to contrast it to the collective form that is so widely familiar to students of world religions. This term, personal ritual, has been necessary in order to stress two central features of the experience of commitment: that it is similar to ritual in being the *acting out* of belief, while at the same time it seems to be realized in the form of personal, not collective, experience. However, as I will demonstrate below, one cannot miss the fact that at Immanuel Church the imagery of salvation is repeatedly formulated in strongly collective terms. The implication is that even this highly personalized form of ritual retains the stamp of collective action. Rather than *being* collective action, personal ritual is oriented toward the *promise* of collective action. It is as if one component of the age-old format of ritual has been split off at Immanuel Church and become the *end* of ritual, with the result that the course of religious life ceases being any form of "stereotyped action" (its own end) and becomes a pursuit, a quest.

I have asserted that the imagery of salvation at Immanuel Church is collective, and indeed the evidence for this claim is overwhelming. For example, I mentioned that salvation is often discussed in the church under the rubric of the "kingdom of God" and that this phrase is consistently associated with living together in harmony and justice with others. Consider the following (paraphrased) comments of a middle-aged widow, a life-long SMF member:

> God's Kingdom is here, in this world everyday. We see it in our relations with others. I can tell you two situations where I'm especially aware of God's kingdom. First, in church almost every Sunday. And second, when I talk to people in day-to-day situations and I feel we really reach one another. When that happens I feel there's been contact and learning, some kind of progress. You experience God's kingdom when you help another person or are helped by another person, when you give another person what they most need, whether that's a word about God or a pair of shoes.

This woman went on to give another example. She mentioned that she often feels a "lift" after talking with another person and that this lift is a sign of the presence of the kingdom of God. She counts the joy that a successful social interaction can bring as a religious feeling.

Other informants mentioned that they feel God's presence in other, widely varying, social situations. For example, one woman said that it is "odd," but she feels closest to God when she is together with young children. The following exchange with a middle-aged woman is a particularly clear representation of this pattern:

Interviewer: When do you feel nearest to God? What do you experience, what does it feel like?

A: Well, I'm probably happiest when I think I've done something *genuine* for another person. It doesn't have to be that I've said something about God, but just that I feel like it was God who helped me. But it *always* concerns a relation to another person. I can get one of these lightning-fast certainties that it was God, it was God's happiness and God's love and all that.

Interviewer: Can you give me an example so I know what you mean?

A: Yeah, it's just when I think I notice that I've made another person happy, either when I give them something or invite them over or say something about God. When I absolutely honestly notice that that person is happy

because of that. *Then,* then I believe in God. Then I think that he's shown himself.
Interviewer: What's your picture of God's kingdom?
A: (pause) It's when people live in love without broken relations to one another. I think that's the kingdom of God.

Such ideas linking sociality and spirituality pervade discourse at Immanuel Church, especially those discussions devoted to the question of the political and social responsibilities of the Christian. The conception of God's kingdom lurks in the background of all such discussions—whether or not it is explicitly mentioned—providing the standard against which social conditions in this world are evaluated. This is clearly illustrated in one of the first speeches I ever heard at Immanuel Church, a lecture to the church youth group by one of SMF's most visible "inspirational poets." This man was a typical example of a not uncommon figure within Protestantism, the devotional leader whose fervor and rather corny enthusiasm cannot be labeled naive because of his well-established status as a former sinner, in this case as an alcoholic.

The poet presented on this particular evening a critique of modern symbolic and material culture. Sweden, he said, has done a good job in the important task of satisfying the material needs—jobs, housing, health—of its citizens. The nation has developed a science based on measurement and technology and, applying these to its people, has discovered that they need certain kinds of things that can be measured. But people also need things that cannot be measured, and here, he said, our society seems to be at a loss. Today, growing social problems such as alcoholism, drug abuse, desperation, and loneliness wrack the nation, but the technocracy that dominates Sweden is at a loss to respond. Its only solution is to offer or promise more material goods. But this will not work, he maintained, because these problems reflect spiritual rather than material needs. It is because of a culture that neglects their spiritual needs that hundreds of thousands of Swedes have been and are being destroyed.

Every person on earth, he claimed, worries about the basic questions of his origin, his present, and his future. These are spiritual problems, problems of the soul, and every person must deal with them. To be isolated, to have no fellowship *(gemenskap)* with others, to be alienated from one's origin and future, this is what happens to those who ignore the spiritual. This is hell, and thousands are in hell in Sweden.

Note the way a series of social problems has been tied here to a spiritual vocabulary. Most obviously, words such as "spiritual," "soul," and "hell" have been used to describe a worldly situation. Consider also the sentence above beginning "to be isolated. . . ." This statement phrases a metaphysical dilemma in terms of a social image. To ignore the spiritual is to be *alienated* and *isolated* from others and from one's origin and future, from one's place in the universe. This is hell, the absence of God. This absence of God is identified at once with a social and metaphysical displacement. The social aspects of this metaphor are explicitly developed in the next section of the speech.

Man's spiritual nature, said the speaker, is responsible for and fulfilled in his sociality. Every person is born with a soul, which is a representation of God within him. In the proper environment, this soul will send out arms, so that in anything the person says or does, the soul will be represented. Of course, the result of a person's saying and doing is to create links to other people: the arms reach out to others. The New Testament tells us that taking care of our souls, the satisfaction of our social needs, is the central problem in our lives. "The meaning of creation is belonging to all things and all people. To be a believer is to be whole."

Thus, the problems of modern Sweden are identified at once with a lack of social contact and a lack of God. The message is the same as that of the middle-class reform movement of a century ago: By bringing God to the people, the society can be healed. But the image of salvation has changed. Before salvation was manifested in a conversion experience the central characteristic of which was turning from a past life of drink and sin; now it is represented by nothing so much as the functioning social bond, that which links one person to another.

Examples of this equation between salvation and sociality could be appended at length, but I will limit myself to one more. As was shown in the second chapter, evangelism has been from the first the *raison d'être* of SMF. The name of the organization, after all, refers to its fundamental character as an institution for mission work. Evangelism was originally understood in SMF to be winning souls for Christ thorough mission activity abroad and revival meetings at home. However, Christian evangelism has also from its very beginnings been understood to entail a component of social reconstruction, and SMF is no exception to this general rule.[3]

In SMF, the social understanding of *evangelist* has always constituted a current of meaning flowing alongside a more narrowly defined spiritual sense of the term. In recent decades, however, there has developed, at least in Immanuel Church, a general agreement that the primary Christian duty evoked by *evangeliet* is broadly social, not narrowly spiritual. In the church's official newspaper I read the following in 1978: "What evangelism means is helping people discover that Christ stands by their side in the struggle against all inhumanity which destroys people's lives and fellowship *(gemenskap)*." The author of the article then cites an official church publication: "Evangelism is a question of listening, loving, and being friends with people."

A perhaps inevitable outgrowth of this "social" understanding of *evangeliet* is that the term takes on a loosely specified political content. As noted in the second chapter, specific political positions are rarely espoused from the pulpit. However, the admonishment to action, the message that Christianity entails an active involvement in the business of improving society is hammered home again and again. The following is the concluding passage from a sermon about Jesus' temptation in the wilderness. It illustrates, one more time, the fervent ambiguity of the call to political action at the same time that it hints at a shift from a personal to a social morality:

> Jesus' temptation is about his not wanting to go that way that was staked out for him. That he did not want to sacrifice and suffer. That he would want to obtain power for himself. And likewise our temptation as Christians is that we forget why we are in the world and what it entails to live in the world as a child of God. And so maybe instead we devote ourselves with all our energies to avoiding vast numbers of temptations that only concern ourselves. [Temptations] that don't really affect anybody else. We wonder, we think, we abstain on a number of different levels. But maybe it's so that at the same time we are so occupied with ourselves, so careful about not succumbing to temptation, we succumb to the biggest temptation of them all: that of forgetting other people. To exist only for our own sake.

Here a personal morality, a concern with the avoidance of sin, is explicitly cited as a potential distraction from that which is really important, the concern for others. Sociality is both the road to and the destination of salvation; the usage of the word *evangeliet* at Immanuel Church further demonstrates the blending of these concepts.

Thus, although salvation is conceived at Immanuel Church as the reception of grace, at the same time salvation is repeatedly discussed in terms of the imagery of collectivity, of sociality. Earlier I spoke of a dual cultural process, a process whose two levels could be named "ritual" and "belief," or "act" and "symbol." Grace and sociality can be understood as the manifestations of salvation, the goal of religious life, on these two different levels. Grace is the process of embodiment or incarnation of beliefs at Immanuel Church; the centrality of sociality is the dominant theme of those beliefs. However, as I have consistently been at pains to stress, the level of belief does not impose itself on the believer; rather, the believer appropriates common images in a personally meaningful process of commitment that is the center of religious life at Immanuel Church.

Another way to put this is to say that at Immanuel Church believers continually *discover* the core image of salvation in terms that are profoundly meaningful to them as persons. In this way a consensus may be formed, but not because it imposes itself upon believers. It will be helpful to return to a believer discussed in an earlier chapter to demonstrate this point.

When, to take a single example, Anders's faith was discussed as exemplifying processes of commitment, the point was that certain symbols of the common faith were extremely salient for Anders because those symbols seemed fused with a pervasive pattern in his thought, a disposition. It may be that Anders found the symbols significant because of the preexisting pattern, or it may also have happened that that pattern crystalized around certain central religious symbols that Anders had adopted. However this congruence arose, the result is the same: There is a portion of the ideological system that is merged with Anders's self.

It therefore transpires that not only does Anders find a profound and touching meaning in these symbols, but—just as important—he finds in the religious system a possibility of self-transcendence. Certain symbols of the faith are at the same time components of Anders's self. In perceiving this equivalence, Anders can see himself in terms of a system of symbols that he shares with other believers; therefore, this transcendence is felt as a direct connection to others who share, or potentially share, the symbols. Thus, in discussing how the church might win converts, Anders says, "What we can offer is community, people who care about one another. That's what is important in the long run, that here we have time for one another, care about one another."

The profound experience of sociality is a *possibility*, a potentiality that may be discovered by the believer who is committed to the faith. Note that this means that one could speak of a source of social cohesion that is not necessarily the result of thought processes of individuals. Group solidarity is incipiently present—whether or not it is discovered—in the process of commitment. I have, then, answered the question posed at the beginning of this chapter, namely, how can commitment contribute to the formation and maintenance of cohesion in a social group? It has been shown that the group may cohere along other dimensions than that of consensus; cohesion is not dependent on the existence of consensus. If church members feel solidarity with their fellows as the result of their experiences of grace, cohesion may be the result not of their agreement but rather of the ongoing processes of commitment.[4]

It follows from this conclusion that it is a mistake to assume, as is often done in critiques of individualism, that the cultural resources necessary to a meaningful sociality are a shared body of traditions, symbols, meanings, or anything else. Rather, the resources for maintaining valid communal life may exist in a group, without that group necessarily adhering to a seamless and compelling orthodoxy. Moreover, although I have made this point by referring to a religious group, I am convinced that secular groups as well as societies as a whole may have access to cultural resources of commitment.

I would like to develop this suggestion somewhat without, of course, embarking on another full-scale analysis. But, given that the problems entailed in individualism are not experienced only by the members of Immanuel Church, it would be surprising if Sweden as a whole were completely without resources that might help its population deal with such problems. It is indisputable, in other words, that as individualism has grown to become the dominant vision of humanity in the West, the possibilities for valid communal experience seem to have diminished throughout those societies. As men and women have come to conceive of themselves ever more as individuals, the stability, warmth, and reassurance of communal forms—of marriage, family, friends, and locality—have become increasingly unavailable. However, the study of Immanuel Church has shown that, for believers there, the experience of community solidarity is alive and well, although hidden from those who assume that this experience must take the form of "consensus" or "stereotyped action." One might suspect, then, that similar resources may be available to groups outside the church, resources which would enable nonbelievers to discover and experience their sociality.

In particular, Sweden as a whole faces precisely the same structural problem that defines so much of what is characteristic about SMF. Although founded on the *form* of a radical and deeply entrenched individualism, it has preserved strong communal values. As economist Robert Heilbroner (1980: 35) wrote recently: "despite its capitalist underpinnings, Sweden is not a capitalist polity. Its ideology is strongly communitarian, albeit mixed with deeply ingrained bourgeois values."

The similarities between SMF and Sweden as a whole are generated not only structurally but historically. The modern Swedish welfare state and the first religious popular movements (*folkrörelser*) were born in the same historical moment and spent their formative years in the same nursery. Both faced the same organizational and moral problem, the forging of solidarity in the face of a professed ideological liberalism. In order to explain these relationships, it will be helpful to return to the set of circumstances that prevailed in Sweden in the latter part of the nineteenth century.

Although modern Sweden was not born in a revolution, it emerged in a time of revolutionary change. At the mid-nineteenth century, Sweden was still a poverty-stricken nation, one of the most backward parts of Europe. Conditions were bad enough so that, over the years between 1850 and 1930, a third of the Swedish population emigrated, mostly to America. However, by the end of this period, the society had been transformed; Swedes were beginning to assemble the modern welfare state that would be universally acknowledged as one of the most prosperous and advanced nations in the world in the period after the Second World War.

Swedish historians have stressed the importance of the *folkrörelser* in effecting this transformation. The grass-roots religious and temperance groups, the workers' movement, and the consumer cooperatives that formed in Sweden in the late nineteenth and early twentieth centuries channeled the aspirations of the people into the organized political activity that was vital to Sweden's development.

The first of the *folkrörelser* to take shape were the religious movements, and SMF—in the sense that it was the first group to actually break with the state church—could be said to have been the earliest of these. It is not surprising, then, that in its early days SMF to some extent served as the organ for forms of revolt other than the strictly religious. This tendency was dramatically illustrated in a well-known episode in Scandinavian labor history, Sweden's first workers' strike, which broke out among sawmill workers in late May of 1879 in the northern town of Sundsvall. It was a depression year following a period of relative prosperity, and, in response to deteriorating business conditions, the sawmill owners lowered wages (Larsson 1972: 39).[5] The workers, who were of course not organized at the time, answered with a spontaneous strike.

The unofficial leader of the strike was a charismatic young worker named Isak Boström. Boström was an active member in a congregation affiliated with the just then emerging SMF, as was another of the three hastily elected leaders of the strike. In the months following the strike, the conservative Swedish press seized on this fact—together with reports that free-church preaching and hymn singing had been observed in the strikers' camp—to argue that free-church agitation was to blame for the strike. Subsequent historiography has stressed that such an interpretation exaggerates the importance of the free churches in these events and ignores the fact that these churches were themselves by and large controlled by middle-class conservatives (see Ohrlander 1977; Larsson 1972). Nevertheless, it is simply indisputable that free-church members, organization, and ideas were a central factor in the strike.[6]

Although the military arrived on the eighth day of the Sundsvall strike to disperse the workers, the tendency for the free churches to serve the ends of nascent social protest was not so easily dissolved. A recently completed study (Åberg 1975) of another northern town, Gävle, in the 1880s concludes that early congregations of SMF were of central importance in the major political transformations that occurred during this period.

As noted, the importance of SMF and other of the *folkrörelser* in the development of modern Sweden has long been recognized. In order to understand the influence of these movements, and particularly those that had a religious basis, it is necessary to have some grasp of the domination of the state church over Swedish society up to the middle of the nineteenth century. Sweden has had a state church as long as it has been a state, a fact which led over the centuries to a certain identification of the two institutions. By 1700 church and state were so intertwined that one had to be baptized in and a member of the church in order to be a Swedish citizen, and state law specified the minimum yearly attendance at communion (Ohlmarks and Gustafsson 1974: 173). Worship services were conceived as not only religious but as civic gatherings, where new regulations and proclamations of the government were passed on to the parish (Löfgren 1980: 197). In addition, prior to 1842, the church provided the structure for local government. The church was very much—in religious, educational, and political senses—at the center of village life (Childs 1980:2, cf. Samuelsson 1968: 168).

In such an atmosphere, dissent from the state church was little different from political revolt (cf. Koblik 1975: 11,12; Davis 1975). In the words of Swedish historian Kurt Samuelsson (1968: 168 – 69): "If a man could read his Bible, believe in *his* God, and serve him as his own conscience, and not authority, dictated, might he not also hold a contrary opinion on mundane matters and dare to express it?" Samuelsson goes on to comment that to conceive of contravening the will of the priest or bishop was furthermore not far from questioning the absolute authority of the agents of secular power. Merely as religious revolt *per se,* then, the free-church movements were the first stages in the transformation of political ideology and organization in Sweden, a process whose end result was the welfare state.

The importance of the free-church movements, however, extends beyond their influence in breaking free of the state church. For example, as groups whose internal organization was democratic, the popular movements worked as a training camp for democracy, their members learning skills and techniques that were then brought to bear on the society as a whole (Johanssen 1952). And their members *did* participate in political activity; witness the study of Gävle (cited above) or the fact that, even today, members of SMF are active in party politics at a rate three times the national average (Zetterberg 1979: Table 5.10).

Another factor that is particularly relevant in this context is the fact that, as Samuelsson (1968: 168) puts it, the free-church movements were the first to preach "the gospel of solidarity and the message of human dignity." Values of temperance or solidarity or the hope for improvement did not spring spontaneously from the lumber camps, the crowded factories, and the slums. Decades before socialism became a vital force in the lives of the Swedish worker, the free churches were vigorously propounding their message.

In significant ways, then, the welfare state of the twentieth century stands on the foundation laid by the *folkrörelser,* especially the religious movements, of which SMF was the largest. The Sundsvall strike is emblematic of the workings of SMF in Swedish social history: the group has been from the first a vital factor in fashioning the unique blend of religious, individualist, and communitarian traditions that comprise the cultural resources of modern Sweden. Historically as well as structurally, then, SMF and Sweden as a whole are similarly located. As a result it might be expected that there are portions of the ideological landscape where SMF and Sweden as a whole blend into one another, where the popular movement that played such an important role in the formation of the modern nation can be viewed as an ideological microcosm of the culture at large.

I would like to tentatively suggest that this is in fact the case, and I will support this suggestion by considering a single element of Swedish secular culture. Here, then, I hope to bring the conclusions of my study of a single congregation to bear on a much larger problem, the analysis of a part of the ideological resources of an entire nation. I do this in part to suggest a possible application of a study such as this one, but also in the hope that any insights gathered outside the walls of Immanuel Church may themselves be subsequently brought to bear on the task of understanding that group.

For all these reasons, then, I will look now at Swedish culture through the lens of a single product of its cultural life. This is the movie "Cries and Whispers," in Swedish *Viskningar och rop,* directed by Ingmar Bergman. Even a fairly quick look at his film will suggest that not only the stress on sociality but several other substantive themes of this study are not limited to SMF.

It should first be mentioned that "Cries and Whispers," in its original Swedish version, is written in a language redolent with biblical and religious overtones. Although the film is not explicitly concerned with God or religion, its language is nevertheless striking in its religious tone. It is not the language of the film as such, however, that I want to address here. Rather, I want to call attention to the manipulation of a few basic—basic to Bergman and basic to Sweden—themes: isolation and social contact, death and love, despair and life.

The four central characters of the film are all women, three of whom (Karin, Agnes, and Maria) are sisters. The fourth is Agnes's servant Anna. The time is the turn of the century, the setting an expansive country house where the sisters were raised. Karin and Maria have left their husbands to be with their unmarried sister in her last days, for she is nearing the end of an agonizing struggle with uterine cancer. In the opening scene, Bergman establishes the fundamental situation of the film: "Three women who are waiting for the fourth to die and take turns to watch by her" (Bergman 1972: 40). Each of the women is associated with a set of images that will be developed and repeated throughout the film. Maria, the youngest of the sisters and her mother's favorite, is beautiful, physical, vain, and outwardly affectionate. Her oldest sister Karin is described by her mental and especially emotional attributes: aloof, cold, and in control. Anna is described (in the screenplay) by one of her most pleasant memories:

> One day, a thunderstorm breaks over the house. Agnes puts on all the lights in the drawing room. Agnes, Anna, and Anna's little daughter dance and build a house under the big dining table. There they are as close as a single body, in common, shuddering enjoyment, undisturbed by the violent storm. In this way, they forget their fear. (Bergman 1972: 40)

As the scenes of the movie unfold, it becomes evident that they are united by a common thread. Each scene depicts the almost capricious giving and withdrawing of affection. Agnes's memory of an encounter with her distant and even cruel mother is a microcosm of the movement in the film as a whole:

> I remember once—it was autumn—I came running into the drawing room; I suppose I had something important to do (one always has at the age of ten). Then I saw Mother sitting there in one of the big chairs. She sat there in her white dress, quite still, looking out the window with her hands resting on the table. She was leaning forward slightly in a peculiar, stiff way. I went up to her. She gave me a look so full of sorrow that I nearly burst into tears. But instead I began to stroke her cheek. She closed her eyes and let me do it. We were very close to each other that time.
>
> Suddenly she came to herself and said, "Just look at your hands, they're filthy. Whatever have you been up to?" Then, overcome with affection, she took me in her arms and smiled at me and kissed me. I was dazzled by these riches. Just as suddenly, she began to weep and begged my forgiveness over and over. I didn't understand a thing; all I could do was hold her tightly until she freed herself. Her face changed and, giving her little laugh, she dabbed her eyes. "How ridiculous," was all she said, then she got up and left me with my tumult. (Bergman 1972: 41 – 42)

The mother's "how ridiculous," the sense of shame and embarrassment both at one's need for interaction and one's feelings of guilt for avoiding it, powerfully expresses the cold decorum so many Swedes feel is dominant in their personalities. The desperate swings between reserve and release that are evidenced in the following agonizing scene between the two healthy sisters are, if in less passionate form, an underlying threat in much of Swedish social life:

> "I want us to be friends," Maria says to Karin. "I want us to touch each other, I want us to talk to each other. After all, we're sisters. We have so many memories in common—we can talk about our childhood! Karin, my dear, it's so strange that we don't touch one another, that we only talk impersonally. Why won't you be my friend? We've been both happy and unhappy, we could hold each other tight. . . . Have I said something to hurt you perhaps? Have I, Karin? It's so easily done, but I swear I didn't mean any harm by it."
>
> . . . Karin shakes her head. "You're wrong," she says with difficulty. "You're wrong, I'm merely afraid."
>
> "What are you afraid of? You're not afraid of me, surely? I don't understand what you mean. Are you afraid to confide in me, don't you trust me? Can't I touch you?"

"No, don't touch me," Karin says. "Don't touch me. I hate any sort of contact. Don't come near me."
. . . Karin begins to weep. It is not pretty weeping; it is violent, ugly, clumsy, with choking sobs and sudden screams.
"I can't," Karin cries, "I can't. All that which can't be altered. All the guilt. It's constant misery and torment. It's like in hell. I can't breathe any more because of all the guilt." (Bergman 1972: 55 – 56)

The film's climactic scene occurs, as so often in Bergman's work, in a sequence that may be a dream or may not, a combination of dream and "real" worlds. Agnes, after her death, returns feebly and briefly to life to beg for help in facing the empty horror of death. She pleads with her sisters and is in turn rebuffed by them:

"I can't," Karin says. "There isn't a soul who'd do what you ask. I'm alive and I don't want anything to do with your death. Perhaps if I loved you. But I don't. What you ask of me is repulsive . . . I'll leave you now. In a few days, I'm going away."
. . . Maria leans closer. She shuts her eyes and face, overcome with cold terror and nausea. Agnes lifts her hand with a somnambulistic movement and removes the combs from Maria's hair. It tumbles down over their faces. Then Agnes puts her hand behind Maria's neck and pulls her violently to her, pressing her lips against Maria's mouth.
Maria screams and wrenches herself away, wiping her mouth with her hand; she staggers backward, spits. then she flees out into the next room. . . . (Bergman 1972: 62 – 64)

In the end it is the servant Anna who calmly stays with Agnes until the terror is past. In the final scene of the movie, the two sisters part after the funeral, accompanied by their respective husbands. Karin makes a desperate attempt to recapture the moment of closeness that followed her outburst above, but Maria refuses to admit that anything of significance has happened.

The movie thus superimposes the image of death over a personal and social struggle that is a pervasive concern in Swedish culture. The intent of this juxtaposition becomes clear in one of the comments Bergman (1976: 86) intersperses with his story: "death is the extreme of loneliness: that is what is so important" (p. 86). Life, on the other hand, is togetherness, as revealed in this passage from Agnes's diary that closes the film:

I closed my eyes and felt the breeze and the sun on my face. All my aches and pains were gone. The people I'm most fond of in the world were with me. I could hear them chatting round about me, I felt the presence of their bodies, the warmth of their hands. I closed my eyes tightly, trying to cling to the moment and thinking: Come what may, this is happiness. I can't wish for anything better. Now, for a few minutes, I can experience perfection. I feel a great gratitude to my life, which gives me so much. (Bergman 1972: 74)

Like Anna's memory of huddling under the table during the thunderstorm— "thus did we overcome our fear," this passage emphasizes that human contact is the only antidote to the existential dilemma of death. Death here is more than the end of biological existence; it is utter loneliness or utter isolation. It is the emptiness, the sensory deprivation feared by many believers at Immanuel Church and classified by them as the essence of evil.

In all these forms, there is but one way of avoiding death: life, the moment of contact with another person. Those who seek a deliverance through tangibles like material possessions or rigid social forms will be condemned to death in life, as are Karin and Maria. The fear of nothingness may bring people to invest their hope for salvation in objects or personal power. But in so doing they neglect that intangible which is the only true solace, the fleeting moment of contact with a fellow human being. Precisely like the speech of the "inspirational poet" that was described above, hell is specified here as isolation (as in Karin's outburst, "it's like in hell") and salvation as the "functioning social bond."

Jesus has been transformed here: he appears, as he so often does at Immanuel Church, in the guise of the encounter with another. But the logic of evil and choice, of salvation from death in this life and the next, and the importance of faith in love remain intact in this transformation.

It is especially in the theme of death that a remarkable parallel emerges. Earlier it was pointed out that the image of salvation at Immanuel Church is very little connected to the problem of death as the end of physical existence, much less so than seems to have been the case a few centuries ago. This fact seems, initially, paradoxical. Observers of Western societies are unanimous in ascribing to modern Westerners a unique horror in the face of death. Although in some ways fascinated with images of violent death, we have in fact removed the actual biological process of death to the furthest reaches of our social life. The existence of the old people's home, the hospital, and the funeral home guarantees that death takes place behind the scenes and intervenes as little as possible into the world of life. It is often remarked (see Stannard 1977: 194; Stannard 1975: vii) that today death has replaced sex as the topic one simply does not talk about, the most shameful of the physical processes. Above all, Westerners are at a loss in the face of death; they "don't know what to say," or, for that matter, to do.

If death is indeed the aspect of life that is most horrible to the modern Westerner, is it not odd that the members of Immanuel Church should to a large extent interpret the rhetoric of salvation as relevant more to life than to death? If these men and women are indeed terrified of death, why do they not concentrate even more than medieval man on that part of the Christian message that guarantees freedom from death?

The answer to this question has already been given by Bergman: death is the extreme of loneliness, and it is *that* that is so important. Death, the cessation of physical existence, is a frightening symbol for a constant threat in the life of modern people, the emptiness of isolation from others. This line of argument leads to the radical conclusion that the profound horror of death that is so obvious in the institutions of Western socieites is in fact a *derived* rather than a direct horror. It is a fear of what death so poignantly symbolizes rather than a fear of the end of life. In an ideological world so devoid of the resources whereby one might conceptualize and celebrate in one's connection to others, the *physical* aspects of that connection—as earlier chapters have shown—take on an increasing importance. The physical is one of the few remaining channels for that which can no longer be said. Thus, the image of the end of physical existence is especially terrifying, for it threatens the end of one of the most tangible means whereby the person might glory in his or her ties to the community.

It is for this reason that the logic of salvation in Immanuel Church no longer refers to life after death. The immediate threat, and the need that this Christian faith has been shown to address, is death in life. In a sense one could say that death has extended its domain and has begun to assert itself in the midst of biological life.[7] This threat is countered not by an abstract philosophy whose *meanings* effectively resolve it, but by resources that allow church members to feel their connection to others and thus live life. These resources are "symbols," but at the same time they are physical experiences that breathe the life of significance into those symbols. On the one hand, a death that can occur before the end of life is transparently a cultural phenomenon, but, on the other hand, it is the physical experience of isolation that lends credence to the identification of "lack of contact" with death. And this cultural system which intertwines death and life with a continuum of "human contact" is by no means, as has just been shown, unique to Immanuel Church; rather, it animates secular products of Swedish expressive life as well.

I began this inquiry with the goal of looking at the social implications of a cultural system in an individualistic context. How, I asked, does ideology work in fostering cohesion in a group that stresses the inevitability of diverse understandings of that ideology? I have attempted to answer this question by directing my attention beyond the level of the meanings attributed by group members to the symbols of their faith to the central experiences of lived faith that believers claim are an essential part of their religion.

In these experiences, which take widely varying forms, I have found a number of common features. Most important is a paradox that stands at the center of these experiences: While the experience of grace is a moment of building the self, a moment of harmony between self-image and the symbols of faith, it is experienced precisely as a moment of going *beyond* the self, an instant of self-transcendence. In a sense this is perhaps not paradoxical, for in order to change the person must necessarily reach beyond the self and take in something that was previously outside it.

This means that the experience of grace, while it may appear individualistic in form, is in fact a moment of communal life appropriated by the believer on a personal level. It is a moment of dwelling within communal symbols, of finding oneself in a picture shared by other members of the group. This is the reason that for many, probably most, members of Immanuel Church the explicit awareness of communal life, the moment of social interaction, is indistinguishable from the process of self-reflection that may occur through the symbols of their faith.

Another common feature of the experience of grace is that the moment of going beyond the self is inevitably manifested as a physical experience. In summary, then, it could be said that the experience of grace is a moment when the self transcends its normal defining boundaries. In order to consider the implications of this fact, it is necessary to review some basic features of the history of the individualistic conception of the self now dominant in Western societies.

Protestantism, and particularly Pietism, arose in a situation of deteriorating orthodoxy. In sanctioning the right, indeed the duty, of the individual to create his or her ideological world, these movements faced an immense problem, that of authorizing or validating such individual outlooks. That is, the old technique of validating ideology—collective ritual—worked through the social process of creating an "authority of numbers" to reinforce the tenets of faith. In a system in which ideology became the responsibility of the individual, a new form of validation became necessary, a form that could be located within the individual.

Thus arose the Pietist emphasis on the *inner* relationship to God, a solution to the problem of validation that entailed the reconceptualization of the soul and the self. The question to ask about the soul was no longer, is it within the embrace of the true church? Rather, qualities intrinsic to the soul became decisive in the question of salvation: Is the soul predestined to salvation? Is it faithful? Has it been transformed through an inner experience of conviction?

In this shift the soul became a different entity, and thus necessarily so did the person; this change is probably the decisive one in the development of the modern Western individual. Divorced from the collectivity and divorced from God, the soul changes from being the part of the person most included to the part most alone, and thus the part most characteristic of what is unique, the individuality. The soul, associated on one hand with God, on the other with individuality, thus confers on the latter a profound value. In this way the need for a new process of validation transformed the person.

The value of the new person is a function of his individuality, his uniqueness. Any relationship to God or to other people is *derived* from this individuality. Thus the new person is ultimately defined by a set of separations: separate from God and separate from the community. There is a third separation, less often remarked, but that has been much in evidence in this study. Individualism seems to entail a separation of the mind from the body.

In this connection, it is suggestive to recall that Descartes was a contemporary of the early Pietist reformers. He too placed an unprecedented stress on the value of an inner process in his renowned *cogito,* the foundation of his metaphysics. And, as is also well-known, his conception of mind entailed an alienation between mind and body that confounds Western thought to this day. In the Cartesian philosophy, this alienation follows from the necessity of insisting on the absolute difference between physical and mental events. However, Western thought as a whole is under no such stricture, yet the Cartesian conception of the absolute separation of mind and body has become its common sense (Cf. Ryle 1949: 11f.).

Although I cannot presume to explain this development, surely it is related in part to the pervasive individualism that characterizes modern thought. The by now diffused influence of Protestantism and various other individualistic ideologies have taught us to regard each self as possessed of a unique inner essence absolutely central to our existence. The Cartesian view of mind and body harmonizes with this supposition by positing a noncorporeal essence within the self, and it is therefore (in part) that such a view has gained widespread acceptance.

Whatever the precise relationship between individualism and the mind-body split, my desire here is merely to emphasize that the testimony and behavior of persons in modern Western societies support the claim that they face a three-fold alienation. The individual is separated from God, from his or her fellows, and from his or her body. The process of grace, or of commitment, at Immanuel Church is the overcoming of these alienations. Grace, for members of Immanuel Church, has three characteristics: it is the moment when the believer is close to God, close to others, and when physical and mental processes merge.

In the introduction I described a widespread set of assumptions about culture that I labeled "culture as consensus." In criticizing those assumptions, I pointed out that "cultural sharing" is, from an empirical standpoint, a rather diffuse notion and that therefore "cultural consensus" is more difficult to demonstrate (or to refute) than is commonly acknowledged. More important, however, was my criticism of "culture as consensus" from a theoretical standpoint. I suggested that "culture as consensus" disguises rather than illuminates the sources and achievement of moral order in society.

In subsequent chapters I have sought to describe how one kind of cultural system, a commitment system, works in the fashioning of a moral order. I have tried to stress that a commitment system is not necessarily an appropriate model for other systems that have an equal right to be termed cultural, such as language or moral strictures. Nevertheless, it seems probable that many cultural systems, and not only in modern societies, may partake of some of the fundamental processes observed in operation at Immanuel Church.

It has been shown how the elements of a cultural system, shared as forms, are attributed meanings on the basis of highly variable personal experience. But this does not entail fragmentation in the group. Rather, it entails a solidarity born of common commitment to a system that each believer conceives as uniquely meaningful to him or her as a person. The processes of symbolic construction of the self mean that each believer is in significant ways literally *composed of* symbolic resources shared among the group as a whole. These processes—which this study has pointed to but hardly begun to investigate—offer a promising approach to the problems of how community is created by, at the same time as it makes possible, human social interaction.

The grand undertakings of the future, however, are not an appropriate subject on which to close such a limited study as this one has been. Rather, I could do no better than to return to my starting point, the sermon of Nils Mjönes, in order to point out that his words about death, on the occasion of his death, take on a new meaning in light of the analysis that has been offered here. In the story he told, the image of death was turned around to symbolize not the absence of grace but its presence, for disappearance was depicted as a *sign* that one had succeeded in painting a perfect image of Jesus. The story says: a perfect faith entails the incarnation of the spirit and this incarnation means the end of the power of death in our lives. Nils Mjönes's original audience listened for spiritual insight, but those whose concern is to understand the modern community may derive something else from the story. The spirit of communities—that which death destroys—is incarnated not where there is perfect consensus but where men and women are able to sustain their faith—that is, to live lives that they find meaningful. This, in any case, is the conclusion one must draw from looking at the workings of grace at Immanuel Church. It is my hope that to understand this much of this one case will provide a foothold for others who wish to further investigate the workings of ideology and the nature of community in modern society.

Notes

Chapter 1: Consensus and Commitment

1. Let me hasten to add that I am not at all confident that social science and religion can be neatly separated. The intellectual foundations of modern social science were laid in an age when, religion having lost much of its unquestioned authority, men and women were searching for a substitute. The thinly disguised religious connections of the word "culture" illustrate a more widespread phenomenon, the fact that several of the key concerns and concepts of social science had their origin in a process of secularization of religious ideas. I will not go into these relationships here; rather I merely wish to cast doubt on the easy assumption that social science and this Swedish religious group stand in a relationship like that between a microscope and a cell.

2. I am by no means the first to question the assumption of cultural sharing; the most widely cited discussion is that of Wallace (1961: 27–39; see also Obeyesekere 1981). Although many of the points I make in my discussion of this issue follow Wallace, I differ from him in an essential point: Although Wallace asserts that neither motivations nor cognitive maps need be shared among members of a society, he does not consider either of these phenomena as within the realm of culture. Culture is that which *is* agreed upon in a society (p. 41), the framework on which diversity is organized, the medium through which business is transacted. Although this is a logical position, it is a position that has been outflanked by subsequent developments in the study of culture. It has come to be accepted that cultural forms work not only to organize activity, but that they in one way or another lend meaning to the existence of those who utilize them. It is this more ambitious conception of culture that I am concerned with in this book,

and thus Wallace's solution to the problem of diversity—the separation of the cognitive from the cultural pattern—is not for me a solution. I agree with those who see culture as a medium through which meaning is organized, and thus I cannot agree that cognitive diversity is not a problem for the theory of culture.

3. It could be disputed that one, say, chooses a religion in a modern society. Some would argue that the conception of choice here is illusory, that in fact such an action is determined by economic factors, psychological factors, or something else. I have no desire to enter into a discussion of the nature of agency in human affairs, so I will simply admit that I *assume* persons make choices. This seems to me a very plausible assumption as assumptions about persons go.

4. By "social cohesion" I mean to designate the valence of those bonds that tie group members to one another and to the group as a whole. Such bonds may be evidenced directly, or by various indirect means, such as commitment to moral strictures that are held by most members of the group.

It may be somewhat surprising to some readers that I would be concerned with social cohesion in a congregation of a church, or perhaps even that I would apply the term "culture" in describing the beliefs, symbols, and ideas of such a group. After all, a congregation is not a society but rather a gathering of selected persons from what we would normally call a society. How then is it legitimate to assume that what goes on at Immanuel Church is in any way analogous to what goes on in a society, whether by that term one means to designate the beloved "primitive" societies of much of anthropology or the enormously complex nation states which are also termed "societies"?

My answer to this question is a simple one. The fundamental postulate of the conception of culture is that the characteristic ideas and ways of proceeding in a group—the culture of a group—has regular and discernible implications for the organization of social life in the group and, by extension, for the activity of members of the group. The gist of this idea lies in the connection between the resources—whether ideational, material, institutional, whatever—available to persons and the life they live. If there is in fact such a connection, it should be evident in *any* social group that endures over time; the issue of political autonomy that seems to lie at the heart of our idea of "society" is peripheral to this fundamental postulate.

Thus I embark on the study of Immanuel Church with the idea that cultural processes—in particular the forging of social cohesion and the influence of cultural resources over the action of group members—will be at work in this group as surely as in the presumably autonomous societies that have more often been the focus of anthropological concern in the past. In fact, it will be explained in the following chapter that Immanuel Church is a group particularly likely to be organized by cultural rather than institutional factors, and in this sense the congregation there is an especially appropriate group in which to observe the social implications of culture.

5. The authors I have cited here agree that the description of behavior is different from culture, but they take different positions on whether culture can be a causal force. Note that I am not, in arguing that culture as description is different from culture as social force, endorsing the position of those who claim that culture never exerts real influence in the social world. I *do* think culture is a force that conditions human action, but I hold it always does so through the medium of practical activity. This means that culture is always being reproduced and transformed by those whom it influences.

6. To meet an obvious but misguided criticism of my position, I should note in no uncertain terms that I am well aware that a, perhaps *the,* fundamental

impetus to the semiotic enterprise is the refusal to construe meaning as a subjective or private phenomenon. In criticizing the idea that meaning is public, I do not mean to endorse the conventional alternative, namely that meaning is private. Meaning is in fact neither social (in the usual sense of that term) nor private but something in between. It is that something in between that I am trying to cast some small amount of light upon in this book.

7. Precisely this point is made, for example, in Fernandez (1965).

8. This distinction was suggested to me by Guy Swanson, personal communication.

9. Other authors have suggested relationships similar to what I am calling commitment here. Compare, for example, Althusser's (1971) conception of ideology. Bourdieu (1977), in suggesting the conception of "doxa," points out that this experience is not available to the level of discourse.

10. This is precisely the point made by Bourdieu (1977), in the first chapter of his *Outline of a Theory of Practice*.

Chapter 2: The Pietist Heritage

1. The idea that Pietism defined itself as an "inner" faith, in contrast to testant orthodoxies, comes from the interesting paper by Meyer (1984).

2. Robert Bellah (personal communication) suggested to me the use of the term "believing in" for the kind of commitment I am referring to here.

3. The imagery of depth which is used here to describe God's word is still very much in evidence at Immanuel Church today, as is demonstrated by the church service that will be described in the following chapter.

4. Frei (1974: 38) apparently agrees with the criticism of Pietism, first advanced in the polemics of the eighteenth century, that its hermeneutics, in being concerned with multiple meanings, was uncontrollable. As the following passage from Gadamer (in the text) should make clear, this criticism is misplaced.

5. See Gustafsson (1968) for an account of Pietism's spread into Sweden.

6. The translation of *förbundet* as "covenant" is in itself problematic, for the word also means union or association. A manufacturer's association, for example, would probably call itself a *förbund*.

7. The transformation of an organization with a charismatic leader to a bureaucracy is the process Weber referred to as the routinization of charisma (see Gerth and Mills 1958: 54).

8. I owe this insight on the importance of lay participation in SMF, as well as my understanding of the relevance of the congregationalist model in this context, to Krister Stendahl (personal communication). I should like to stress, however, that Dr. Stendahl is in no way responsible for any errors in my analysis here.

9. The Swedish word that I have translated here as "interest in social matters" is *samhällstillvändet*, literally "turned toward society." The Swedish word for turn (the verb) is *att vända*, and for convert (as in conversion experience), *omvända*. That is, Swedish preserves in the notion of conversion the image of "turning" that our word has lost. As a result, in Swedish there is a relatively large possibility for word play on the notion of conversion, and this possibility is often seized at Immanuel Church. Here, for example, I would imagine that the author is delivering an underhanded blow at those who think one can be "converted to society."

10. Compare Robert Bellah's (1970) paper.

Chapter 3: Immanuel Church

1. This statistic comes from the Swedish Institute, in a pamphlet published in 1979.

2. I calculated this figure as follows: According to Religionssociologiska Institutet (1969: 2), in 1966, 2.8 percent of the Swedish people were in the state churches on any given Sunday. Since 95 percent of the population in Sweden are members of the state church, it follows that $0.028/0.95 = .0295$, or approximately 3 percent, is the percentage of state church members in church on a Sunday morning.

3. The figures I have cited here are only roughly comparable; for one thing the first is based on attendance, the second on self-reports of attendance. Nevertheless, the comparison is striking and confirms what even a casual observer notices: what religious interest there is in Sweden is disporportionately centered in the free churches.

4. Throughout the book I have largely ignored a question that is certainly important, and overwhelmingly important to many of my colleagues in social science—that of how representative my informants and experiences in this church are. I have not used sampling techniques that would allow me to say that my results are generalizable within the congregation. The reason I have not used such techniques is a purely pragmatic one. I could not do intensive interviews about religious faith with persons selected at random, i.e., people I did not know. I tried it and it did not work; people were uncomfortable discussing these rather personal matters with a stranger. Thus, I was confronted with the choice of getting the information I wanted from people who cannot be claimed to perfectly represent the congregation, or of not getting the information I wanted but being able confidently to claim generalizability (to a single congregation of SMF) for my, to me, insignificant findings. I chose the former strategy; my apologies and sympathy go out to those who would have chosen the latter. For what it is worth, it is my judgment that the wide range of people interviewed by my research assistant and myself give a fair picture of the different sorts of people who attend Immanuel Church.

5. By "liberal" I mean non-socialist (bourgeois). In America, the word is often ambiguously used to refer to any position on the political left of center. I am not following this usage; I mean to contrast liberal values to socialist ones.

6. The stricture against firm political positions is presumably flexible. Church officials, to take an imaginary example, would claim that great evils—such as, say, fascism—should be condemned from the pulpit.

7. The text of Psalm 130 as given in the Revised Standard Version of the Bible is:

Out of the depths I cry to thee, O Lord!
Lord hear my voice! Let thy ears be attentive to the voice of my supplications!
If thou, O Lord, shouldst mark iniquities, Lord, who could stand?
But there is forgiveness with thee, that thou mayest be feared.

8. I have adopted a format similar to the one specified by Dennis Tedlock (1971) for the presentation of the spoken texts in this service. In an attempt to preserve as much of the spoken cadence as possible, I have broken lines whenever the speaker pauses. This mode of transcription means that the lines end with the English equivalents of the Swedish words that preceded the pauses, except in the

very few cases when this would have been incompatible with grammatical English. Here and throughout the book, italics—with no further explanation—indicate speakers' emphasis. My own emphasis is always specified as such.

9. The Swedish word I have translated as "powerlessness" here is *vanmakt,* which also means "unconciousness" and "impotence."

10. The story of Noah can be read in the Bible in Genesis 6 and 7.

11. The Swedish word I have translated here as "the deep abyss" is *avgrundsdjupet.*

Chapter 4: Symbols Without Meaning

1. The Swedish here is *"vigas till,"* which can also mean "to be consecrated to."

2. George Lakoff and Mark Johnson (1980: ix) make a similar distinction between meaning and meaningfulness in their book *Metaphors We Live By.*

3. All but one of the interviews cited in this book were recorded on tape. About two-thirds of the interviews on which this book is based were conducted by my research assistant, Roland Strand (I conducted the rest). I found that my most successful interviews were the ones with believers I knew well, but I was close to only a small number of church members. Roland, a long-time church member, had extensive contacts in the church and an excellent understanding of my project (derived in part through many hours of conversation with me, in part through his extensive background in anthropology). I therefore asked him to do interviews with a number of church members who were outside my immediate circle of acquaintances.

Chapter 5: Discovering the Self

1. SMU stands for *Svenska Missionsförbundets Ungdom,* "Svenska Missionsförbundet's Youth."

2. The equation of contact with God with "openness" in some form is extremely widespread, both in SMF (Per and Anders both mention it, as does Nils, a believer described later in this chapter) and in wider contexts, such as the descriptions of divine contact offered by Luther and Augustine.

3. The position that what I am calling a disposition may be a pattern that pervades thought is consistent with Bourdieu's usage (Bourdieu 1977: 15).

4. A somewhat similar "unusual solution" is entailed in the school of thought known as "process theology." (See, for example, Cobb and Griffin 1976.)

5. To say that Kristina and Anders share certain important outlooks is not to contradict my stated position that sharing is an inadequate basis on which to build a theory of culture. My point has never been that elements of ideology are rarely shared among adherents of the ideology. Rather, it is, first, that the extent of ideological sharing in a group is an empirical problem and, second, that there is no reason to assume that the efficacy of culture is mediated only through shared meanings.

6. My reference to Kristina's profound respect for individuality should not be taken as implying that she propounds an American style of individualism, for

the opposite is the case. She is very careful to stress, when speaking of the possibilities of the individual, that self-realization can occur only in a social context, through working with others.

7. My use of "convert" in this context (themes of thought being "converted" to somatic expressions) may, for some readers, recall Freud's formulation of conversion hysteria. Freud spoke of the physical manifestations of hysteria, which are termed conversion, as the physical symbolization of repressed desires. As far as I can tell, this parallel is coincidental; that is, there is no historical relation between the use of the word "conversion" in evangelical Christianity and its use in psychoanalysis.

Chapter 6: Grace and the Foundation of Experience

1. Some readers will perhaps be appalled by my assertion that meaning is not public and will imagine that it has somehow escaped my notice that words have conventional meanings, that language is a system that exists in some sense beyond any individual speaker, and so on. These facts have not escaped my notice. However, none of them justify the conclusion that symbols in any strict sense carry their meanings. Meaning is always the result of the interaction of a human being and a socially generated symbol, and it is obviously wrong to leave the human being out of this relation.

2. Roland, my research assistant, did this interview; he has a carefully cultivated capacity to express himself colorfully.

3. The formulation Maryann is using here seems to be based on Psalm 115, quoted in part in the following text.

4. Compare, for example, the preceding footnote. It seems to be psalmic formulations that are particularly important to Maryann.

5. Lena is referring here to the sermon on the mount: "You are the salt of the earth. . . . You are the light of the earth" (Mathew 5: 13, 14, New English Bible).

6. Reports of feelings of "emptiness" are common among men and women who are seriously depressed, according to mental-health professionals to whom I have spoken about Anna's interview.

Chapter 7: The Image of Salvation

1. As was noted in the third chapter, the single criterion for membership in SMF is "confession of faith in Jesus Christ as Lord and Saviour."

2. The most basic facts of Luther's life and character point unambiguously to this conclusion. See, for example, the entire first chapter of Bainton's (1950) popular biography of Luther, *Here I Stand.*

3. R. H. Tawney (1954: 24) wrote that evangelism, the mission of the church, has always been understood as entailing attending to the needs of the society as a whole:

> The church of the earlier middle ages had been engaged in an immense missionary effort, in which as it struggled with the surrounding barbarism, the work of conversion and of social reconstruction had been almost indis-

tinguishable. By the very nature of its task, as much as by the intention of its rulers, it had become the greatest of social institutions. For good or evil it aspired to be not a sect, but a civilization, and, when its unity was shattered at the Reformation, the different churches which emerged from it endeavored, according to their different opportunities, to perpetuate the same tradition.

4. My point that group solidarity may be based in processes of commitment is, given the way I have defined the term, similar to Freud's (1951) contention that a group may be based in shared identifications. See Ricoeur (1970: 512 – 13) for a discussion of this point.

5. Ohrlander (1977: 25) says that wage reductions were on the order of 15 – 20 percent. This is the only place I have seen such a figure.

6. The tendency in European history for Protestant reform to serve the ends of social reform is often remarked. Classic works, however, may have underestimated the complexity of this process. See Davis (1975).

7. Bernhard Anderson (1974: 89), in the book on the psalms cited earlier, discusses the idea of "death in life" as a part of the cosmology of ancient Israel.

Bibliography

Åberg, Ingrid
   1975   Förening och politik. Folkrörelsernas politiska aktivitet i Gävle
          under 1880-talet. Uppsala: Acta Universitatis Upsaliensis.
Althusser, Louis
   1971   Ideology and Ideological State Apparatuses (Notes towards an
          Investigation). In *Lenin and Philosophy and Other Essays*.
          127 – 86. New York: Monthly Review Press.
Anderson, Bernhard W.
   1974   *Out of the Depths: The Psalms Speak for Us Today*. Philadelphia:
          The Westminster Press.
Andersson, Axel
   1914   Kristendomen och den sociala frågan. SMU småskrifter No. 9.
          Stockholm: Svenska Missionsförbundet Förlag.
   1934   Svenska Missionsförbundet. In *De frikyrkliga samfunden i
          Sverige*. Gunnar Westin, N.J. Nordström, Jonathan Julen and
          Axel Andersson, 143 – 78. Stockholm: Svenska Missionsför-
          bundet Förlag.
Augustine, St.
   1961   *Confessions*. Baltimore: Penguin Books.
Bainton, Roland H.
   1950   *Here I Stand: A Life of Martin Luther*. Nashville: Abingdon
          Press.
   1956   *The Age of the Reformation*. Princeton: D. Van Nostrand
          Company.

Balint, Enid
  1963 On Being Empty of Oneself. *International Journal of Psychoanalysis* 44: 470 – 80.

Bellah, Robert N.
  1970 Transcendence in Contemporary Piety. In *Beyond Belief: Essays on Religion in a Post-Traditional World,* 196 – 208. New York: Harper & Row.

Bergman, Ingmar
  1972 Cries and Whispers. *The New Yorker* 48 (October 21, 1972): 38 – 74.
  1976 *Four stories by Ingmar Bergman.* Garden City: Doubleday/Anchor Books.

Boas, Franz
  1889 On Alternating Sounds. *American Anthropologist* 2: 47 – 53.

Bourdieu, Pierre
  1977 *Outline of a Theory of Practice.* Cambridge: Cambridge University Press.

Burke, Kenneth
  1973 *The Philosophy of Literary Form. Studies in Symbolic Action.* 3rd Ed. Berkeley: University of California Press.

Childs, Marquis W.
  1980 *Sweden: The Middle Way on Trial.* New Haven: Yale University Press.

Cobb, John B., Jr., and David Ray Griffin
  1976 *Process Theology: An Introductory Exposition.* Philadelphia: The Westminster Press.

Davis, Natalie Z.
  1975 Strikes and Salvation at Lyon. In *Society and Culture in Early Modern France,* 1 – 16. Stanford: Stanford University Press.

Dumont, Louis
  1965 On Individualism. *Contributions to Indian Sociology* 8: 13 – 61.

Durkheim, Emile
  1915 *The Elementary Forms of the Religious Life.* New York: The Free Press.

Fernandez, James W.
  1965 Symbolic Consensus in a Fang Reformative Cult. *American Anthropologist* 67: 902 – 29.

Francke, August Hermann
  1969 *August Hermann Francke: Werke in Auswahl.* Erhard Peschke, ed. Berlin: Evangelische Verlagsanstalt.

Frei, Hans W.
  1974 *The Eclipse of Biblical Narrative. A Study in Eighteenth and Nineteenth Century Hermeneutics.* New Haven: Yale University Press.

Freud, Sigmund
 1951   *Group Psychology and the Analysis of the Ego.* New York: Liveright Publishing Co.
Gadamer, Hans-Georg
 1975   *Truth and Method.* New York: Continuum.
Geertz, Clifford
 1973   *The Interpretation of Cultures.* New York: Basic Books.
 1983   *Local Knowledge: Further Essays in Interpretive Anthropology.* New York: Basic Books.
Gerth, Hans, and C. Wright Mills, eds.
 1958   *From Max Weber: Essays in Sociology.* New York: Oxford University Press.
Giddens, Anthony
 1971   *Capitalism and Modern Social Theory: An Analysis of the Writings of Marx, Durkheim and Max Weber.* Cambridge: Cambridge University Press.
Goodenough, Ward H.
 1981   *Culture, Language and Society.* 2nd Ed. Menlo Park, California: The Benjamin/Cummings Publishing Company.
Gunkel, Hermann
 1928   *Einleitung in die Psalmen; die Gattungen der Religiösen Lyrik Israels.* Göttingen: Vanderhoeck and Ruprecht.
Gustafsson, Berndt
 1957   *Svensk Kyrkohistoria.* Stockholm: Verbum.
 1968   Sekulariseringen ur religionssociologisk aspekt. Forskningsrapport nr 51, Religionssociologiska Institutet i Stockholm. (mimeo).
Heilbroner, Robert L.
 1980   The Swedish Promise. *New York Review of Books* 27: 33 – 36.
Hobbes, Thomas
 1958   *Leviathan.* Indianapolis: The Bobbs-Merrill Company. [orig. 1651]
Johanssen, Hilding
 1952   *Folkrörelserna och det demokratiska statskicket i Sverige.* Stockholm: Gleerups.
Koblik, Steven
 1975   Introduction. In *Sweden's Development from Poverty to Affluence 1750 – 1970*, 3 – 13. Steven Koblik, ed. Minneapolis: University of Minnesota Press.
Kroeber, A. L., and C. Kluckhohn
 1963   *Culture: A Critical Review of Concepts and Definitions.* New York: Vintage Books.
Lakoff, George, and Mark Johnson
 1980   *Metaphors We Live By.* Chicago: University of Chicago Press.

Larsson, Tage
1972   *Väckelsen och Sundsvallsstrejken 1879*. Stockholm: Gummesons.

Lévi-Strauss, Claude
1969   *The Raw and the Cooked*. New York: Harper and Row.

Löfgren, Orvar
1980   Historical Perspectives on Scandinavian Peasantries. *Annual Review of Anthropology* 9: 187 – 215.

Meagher, Paul Kevin, Thomas C. O'Brien, and Sister Consuelo Maria Aherne
1979   *Encyclopedic Dictionary of Religion*. Washington D.C.: Corpus Publications.

Meyer, Elizabeth
1984   The Halle Pietists: Unmasking Religious Truth. Unpublished manuscript, files of the author.

Nicklasson, Gösta
1978   *En Kristen livsrörelse*. Stockholm: Gummesons.

Obeyesekere, Gananath
1981   *Medusa's Hair: An Essay on Personal Symbols and Religious Experience*. Chicago: University of Chicago Press.

Ohlmarks, Åke, and Berndt Gustafsson
1974   *Svenskarnas religion: från istiden till våra dagar*. Stockholm: A. B. Tryckmans.

Ohrlander, Gunnar
1977   *Hoppets Här*. Stockholm: Ordfront.

Parsons, Talcott
1968   *The Structure of Social Action*. New York: The Free Press.

Pinson, Koppel S.
1934   *Pietism as a Factor in the Rise of German Nationalism*. New York: Columbia University Press.

Religionssociologiska Institutet i Stockholm
1969   Smärre Meddelanden 1. (mimeo).

Ricoeur, Paul
1970   *Freud and Philosophy: An Essay in Interpretation*. New Haven: Yale University Press.

Ryle, Gilbert
1949   *The Concept of Mind*. New York: Barnes and Noble.

Sammuelsson, Kurt
1968   *From Great Power to Welfare State: 300 Years of Swedish Social Development*. London: George Allen and Unwin.

Schneider, David
1968   *American Kinship: A Cultural Account*. Englewood Cliffs, New Jersey: Prentice-Hall.

Sperber, Dan
  1974   *Rethinking Symbolism.* London: Cambridge University Press. [English Language Edition 1975].
Stannard, David E.
  1975   Introduction. In *Death in America,* vii – xv. Philadephia: The University of Pennsylvania Press.
  1977   *The Puritan Way of Death: A Study in Religion, Culture, and Social Change.* New York: Oxford University Press.
Stocking, George W. Jr.
  1982   *Race, Culture and Evolution: Essays in the History of Anthropology.* 2nd. Ed. Chicago: University of Chicago Press.
Stoeffler, F. Ernest
  1965   *German Pietism during the Eighteenth Century.* Leiden: E. J. Brill.
  1971   *The Rise of Evangelical Pietism.* Leiden: E. J. Brill.
Stromberg, Peter
  1981a Religious Language and Personal Ethics in a Swedish Church. Ph.D. dissertation, Department of Anthropology, Stanford University.
  1981b Consensus and Variation in the Interpretation of Religious Symbolism: A Swedish Example. *American Ethnologist* 8: 544 – 59.
  1985   The Impression Point: Synthesis of Symbol and Self. *Ethos* 13: 56 – 74.
Swartz, Marc
  1982   Cultural Sharing and Cultural Theory: Some Findings of a Five-Society Study. *American Anthropologist* 84: 314 – 38.
Tawney, R. H.
  1954   *Religion and the Rise of Capitalism, a historical study.* New York: New American Library.
Tedlock, Dennis
  1971   On the Translation of Style in Oral Narrative. *Journal of American Folklore* 84: 114 – 33.
Tylor, Edmund
  1889   *Primitive Culture.* New York: Henry Holt and Co.
Walan, Bror
  1878   *Året 1878.* Stockholm: Gummesons.
Wallace, Anthony F. C.
  1961   *Culture and Personality.* New York: Random House.
Weber, Max
  1930   *The Protestant Ethic and the Spirit of Capitalism.* New York: Charles Scribner's Sons.
Wennås, Olof
  1978   *Liv och Frihet: En bok om Svenska Missionsförbundet.* Stockholm: Gummesons.

Williams, Raymond
  1983   *Culture and Society: 1780–1950*. 2nd. Ed. New York: Columbia
         University Press.
Zetterberg, Hans L., et al.
  1979   *Frikyrkosverige: ett livsstilsstudie*. Stockholm: A. B. Realtryck.

Index